A Citizen's Guide
to Grassroots
Campaigns

A Citizen's Guide to Grassroots Campaigns

Jan Barry

Rutgers University Press

New Brunswick, New Jersey, and London

Library of Congress Cataloging-in-Publication Data

Barry, Jan, 1943–
   A citizen's guide to grassroots campaigns / Jan Barry.
      p. cm.
   Includes bibliographical references and index.
   ISBN 0–8135–2800–3 (cloth : alk. paper)—ISBN 0–8135–2801–1
   (pbk. : alk. paper)
   1. Political activists—New Jersey. 2. Political participation—
   New Jersey. I. Title.
   JK3589.B37 2000
   323'.042'09749—dc21   99–056790

British Cataloging-in-Publication data for this book is available from
the British Library

Manufactured in the United States of America

Dedicated
to all good people
who see a problem,
roll up their sleeves,
and take constructive action

Contents

Preface

I'm a journalist, a war veteran, a parent—and, when push comes to shove, a civic activist. Guess which is the hardest job. Democracy is a lot harder to *do* than it is to talk about or fight over. Infused with the democratic spirit the United States is celebrated for, Americans often enthusiastically back a cause, from animal rights to world peace. Such enthusiasm too often turns sour. Jumping into civic affairs, people find that little in their education prepared them for the real thing. Fledgling activists, unless fortunate in their networking and lucky in surviving missteps, soon discover how difficult it is to accomplish much when fiery emotions and good intentions are not harnessed by skillful organizing. The aim of this book is to provide the distilled expertise of experienced civic action organizers and tips on becoming one.

The focus of this guidebook is on citizen campaigns in America's most urbanized and yet very diverse state, New Jersey—the Garden State, where civic action flourishes like tomato vines. In a state once maligned as a malodorous turnpike between New York and points south, citizen groups have repeatedly demonstrated a mastery of grassroots civic campaigns—establishing community recycling projects that created an effective alternative to the state's infamous garbage mounds; saving scenic wonders of wilderness from being paved over; rebuilding blighted urban neighborhoods; organizing mutual-help groups that transformed lives; helping reveal the health threat of Agent Orange; tackling the threat of nuclear war and helping transform Russia from a frightening enemy into a trading partner. The diverse civic actions on local, national, and international issues featured in this book provide windows on another America—one in which citizens set the agenda.

That's not to say everything citizens do is covered in this book. Or that engaging in citizen action guarantees success. There are all kinds of actions by disparate groups: civil rights campaigns, protests of civil rights claims, teacher strikes over salary contracts, taxpayer protests over rising taxes, civil disobedience at military bases by war protesters, petition tables manned by military supporters promoting antimissile defenses, massing of shoes representing gunshot victims, planting crosses representing abortion deaths, flag-waving veterans marching to a war memorial, flag-burning protesters marching on a federal building, pickets against the death penalty, pickets for the death penalty. Exercising a tradition that a Martian might view with amazement, Americans frequently mount rallies, marches, and other actions to promote diametrically opposed pronouncements by various religious, racial, ethnic, social, or regional groups. Public spaces, from the Mall in Washington to city halls and Main Streets nationwide, are in many ways living bulletin boards where clashing statements on virtually any issue are posted. The net effect is often a tense seesawing balance of pressures by competing interest groups—out of which have come grudging compromises or a happier sense of well-aired consensus that create a vibrant society many people in other nations envy.

To me, all that ferment is what makes life in America more interesting, more creative, and more livable than many other places. Having seen the alternative in Vietnam, I much prefer to see competing groups of people contending in the civic arena rather than battling it out with bullets and bombs, leaving a legacy of bitterness and a mine-strewn deadly landscape. That's why the focus of this book is on the role of civic groups in creating the places where we live or visit for recreation. Over the years, I've seen many activists sorely frustrated as much by the process as with the outcome of participation in civic affairs. Citizen activists generally learn by trial and error. If they are lucky, they get helpful advice from old-timers who've "been there, done that." The aim of this book is to offer practical know-how gleaned from the hard-won experience of an array of activists involved in civic projects that reached their goals, or by those who came close and were encouraged by the results to continue the campaign.

The examples I chose are citizen-organized campaigns that sought broad-based civic involvement and public dialog for a community, regional, or international cause that would benefit most people regardless of their political, social, or religious beliefs. These are campaigns, often in areas where government agencies had been stymied, in which citizens reached out across the divisions in America to promote actions that could only be successful with broad civic participation and that afterward became an important component of the American landscape or society. The case studies presented here are representative of various types of civic campaigns. There are many others. This is not a comprehensive history of civic activism in New Jersey. Nor is it a social critique of what's wrong in American society. It is an examination of what, sometimes, works. These examples offer modest but durable lessons in how citizen campaigns transform individual concerns into community action.

The conclusions in this book are solely my own, one citizen's observations drawn from a few strands in Americans' incredibly varied, interwoven, and invaluable civic life.

They are drawn from civic campaigns I've covered as a journalist and observed as an interested citizen, as well as from my own experiences as an activist on two issues of war or peace I felt compelled to try to tackle.

The idea to write such a book grew from studies at Ramapo College of New Jersey's School of American and International Studies, where I completed a degree in political science at an advanced age, thanks to a state scholarship for Vietnam veterans. In discussions with classmates who did volunteer work for an astonishing variety of causes and with international students from nations struggling to develop democracies, who asked how grassroots civic action in America works, I wished there were a book I could quote that presented, instead of political theories, practical information that people had developed while doing a neighborhood project or waging an international campaign. I wished there were a concise how-to guide that explained the dynamics of actual citizen campaigns. As a journalist with some previous experience as a civic activist, I decided to see what I could do. Little did I realize it would take the better part of a decade.

The first seeds of this project were also sown long ago. I was raised in rural upstate New York in the Eisenhower era on the tenets of the Boy Scouts, Protestant Sunday school, and American Legion Boys State, and my concept of public service upon graduating from high school in 1961 was joining the army. My awakening to civic alternatives began when I was a GI in Vietnam. From the perspective of a private first class in an aviation unit that operated Canadian bush-pilot planes to transport Special Forces teams in and out of remote jungle outposts, I felt we should have sent the Peace Corps, rather than military forces, to solve the region's real problems. As Vietnamese factions clashed over what kind of society—capitalism, communism, or tradition-oriented Buddhist culture—should replace French colonialism, the U.S. government's contribution to that cultural and political debate was to raze ancient villages with bombs and napalm.

While the Reverend Dr. Martin Luther King Jr. was being lionized at home for leading a civil rights movement that was protected by federal troops when violent opponents threatened its members, Vietnamese Buddhists who marched in peaceful demonstrations in South Vietnam were assaulted by government troops armed and trained by the U.S. military. Official explanations that GIs were in Vietnam to protect the Vietnamese people rang hollow. We certainly didn't treat them as American citizens active in political issues were treated at home. After being appointed from the ranks to the United States Military Academy, I rebelled and resigned from a military career. The deceitful, undemocratic decision making that characterized U.S. foreign policy in Southeast Asia seemed to me to be undermining American ideals. As the army chain of command discouraged soldiers from expressing their own views, I felt my civic duty lay in leaving West Point and writing an expose of what was then a distant, secretive military operation in Indochina.

Trading my rifle for a typewriter, I discovered effective writing requires skills I struggled to learn. Fuming over the massive bombing and ground-war escalation in Vietnam, Cambodia, and Laos that caused horrendous civilian casualties and numbing numbers of GI deaths no matter what anyone wrote, I dashed off a blistering letter blasting that senseless military misadventure and returned my war medals to the Pentagon. The mail brought no reply. Infuriated at being ignored, I joined a peace march to the United Nations headquarters in New York, despite inner panic at becoming a public spectacle. The war roared on. What began as a statement of personal dissent turned into a four-year stint as a founder of Vietnam Veterans Against the War, the first national organization of veterans of that war. Like many other Americans, I got a crash course in the ordeal of citizens challenging their own government over war policy. The main lesson, which was hard to accept, was harsh: no matter what anyone did, war seemed impervious to all protests.

Given American history's focus on warfare as an activity that forged a nation, expanded its frontiers, and crowned it a world superpower, there were no helpful models for stopping a war. We small band of veterans joined with other peace activists because we believed the American people were capable of debating issues, reaching a reasonable conclusion, and changing government policy. Given the ineffectual anarchy of the peace movement and the blind, brutal mind-set in the government, the war in Indochina ground on and on to a disastrous end in 1975, leaving a bitter aftertaste throughout America and Southeast Asia. Many of us dropped out of 1960s-style activism long before the bitter end, disillusioned with both antiwar protests and military service.

Some disgusted alumni of that dismal era of dissent rethought their role as citizens who took democracy seriously; they regrouped and created better-organized campaigns. A wholly different peace movement emerged in the 1980s and 1990s. Taking a cue from the environmental movement, it merged grassroots organizing and global issues. One project, sparked by Vietnam veterans and a wide spectrum of other people, created the International Campaign to Ban Landmines, which fostered a global treaty that was signed by most of the world's governments; the group and its coordinator, Jody Williams, were awarded the 1997 Nobel Peace Prize for that effort.

Another project, in which I, along with many others,

exorcised Vietnam-era ghosts, created a citizen diplomacy campaign that hosted Soviet-American exchange visits and sister-city ties with our nuclear missile–armed adversaries. In that campaign, many peace activists learned the value of engaging government officials in diplomatic dialog as well as public debate. It was a far more sophisticated level of citizen activism than the often counterproductive, bitter protests of the 1960s, and the citizen diplomacy campaign of the 1980s played a major role in the end of the Cold War. It was a campaign with a historic outcome, and it transformed seemingly powerless inhabitants of hostile military blocs into savvy world citizens.

That experience planted another seed of this book project. As a community and state organizer of that citizen diplomacy campaign, I traveled with other volunteers to the Soviet Union to meet with civic groups in Russia, Estonia, and Soviet Georgia—places I had never expected to visit in my life. I found myself hosting Soviet exchange visitors to New Jersey, who were greeted in community after community as the key to helping us all survive the looming threat of global "nuclear winter" destruction. And I helped create sister-city ties and educational, cultural, and business exchanges that blossomed in the 1990s. This was a very different sort of creative work than my life as a writer.

I gained additional insight into effective organizing while working, during several years of the citizen diplomacy campaign, as a public information officer for the National Board of the YWCA of the U.S.A., which has decades of experience teaching mutual-aid and community-action organizing skills to women in American small towns and big cities, as well as overseas. After my army experience, it was refreshing to write newsletters, brochures, and press kits describing how YWCA members and staff (who come from a wide variety of ethnic, racial, and economic backgrounds) mobilize diverse people from teenagers to corporate executives to create interwoven networks that tackle issue after issue at community, regional, national, and international levels. The issues these women and male supporters tackle range from providing quality child care to working toward preventing global wars and improving life for women and children in Third World countries and impoverished American neighborhoods.

As many people do, I found the relentless pace of activism exhausting. Juggling my public relations job in New York with organizing a civic movement in New Jersey while raising two rambunctious children with my equally busy wife, an international business executive, I reached a point where I was burned out, my life frazzled. Furthermore, the threat of nuclear war that so worried me dissipated as American and Soviet leaders embraced the spirit of the citizen diplomacy campaign and began seriously negotiating about how to dismantle the hair-trigger war machinery poised to destroy each other's country. When health problems warned me to slow down, I returned, equipped with new insights into citizen campaigns, to the work I most enjoy, writing for newspaper readers.

Shortly after the Vietnam War ended, looking for a day job to support a poetry-writing habit, I had drifted into covering municipal council and school board meetings for a daily newspaper. Amid the droning boredom, a dramatic interaction of citizens and officials would quite often erupt in face-to-face debate, which in turn would sometimes transform into a mutually respectful discussion of serious issues. When I began research for this book project, casting about for exemplary cases to cite, I realized there were excellent examples all around me. Working as a news reporter in New Jersey off and on for nearly twenty years, I have attended numerous community meetings and public events, recording highlights of civic campaigns focused on local, regional, national, and international issues. It has been a wonderful education, one that was not provided in my college political science books.

My hope is that this book will prove useful for community-minded New Jersey residents, multitudes of other Americans, and people of good will around the world.

Acknowledgments

I'm indebted to many people for inspiration and assistance in putting together this book, especially everyone who was interviewed or quoted from other sources. These are the real experts. My research on grassroots groups relied on news articles and features in the *(Bergen) Record*, the *Star-Ledger*, the *New York Times*, the *Montclair Times*, and other newspapers, the Internet, Montclair State University's Harry A. Sprague Library, and my own files compiled as a journalist and citizen diplomacy organizer. I'm grateful for the faith in this project that my editor, Marlie Wasserman, director of Rutgers University Press, had from the beginning, as well as the enthusiastic encouragement of D. Michael Shafer, professor of political science at Rutgers. I very much appreciate Willa Speiser's incisive copyediting. I also appreciate the constructive criticism by an anonymous reviewer of an early draft of this book, as well as insightful comments by Malcolm A. Borg, publisher of the *Record* and a Palisades Interstate Park commissioner; H. Bruce Franklin, professor of English and American Studies at Rutgers-Newark; and Thomas W. Nusbaumer, an inveterate organizer for Common Cause and other progressive causes.

I'm also indebted to my assignment editor at *The Record*, Claude Deltieure, for guiding me to develop a stylish yet thoroughgoing mode of reporting; he encouraged me to relentlessly dig beyond official statements and show the dramatic interaction of citizens and officials in addressing contentious, vital issues, while conveying the relevant facts and viewpoints in each case. I'm grateful to Elizabeth K. Parker, editor of *Environment New Jersey*, for commissioning in-depth articles on environmental issues, organizations, and organizers that provided much of the material for chapter 3. I very much appreciate the sacrifices my wife, Paula, made so I could write this book.

A Citizen's Guide to Grassroots Campaigns

1

Citizens

in Action

Civic movements are America's internal combustion engine. They also play a vital role around the world. Internationally, nonprofit groups operated and financed by private citizens in the United States and other nations distribute more aid to disaster victims than does the World Bank, according to the Associated Press. Citizen groups are often providing aid at a disaster scene while governments are still negotiating aid packages. "Private organizations increasingly play roles once considered the preserve of governments," the *New York Times* noted in another report on this phenomenon, which includes overseeing elections, pressing peace treaties, and environmental protection. In the United States, nearly one-third of disaster relief is handled by nonprofit agencies that mobilize private donations and volunteer efforts of countless concerned citizens. Name a health concern, environmental issue, or civil rights case: the lead in taking action was set, most often, by citizen groups.

The United States of America began in a revolution over the rights of people to act in their own interest. As Thomas

Paine thundered in *The Crisis*, that fiery call to revolt against the restrictions of colonial life conceived while he was tramping across New Jersey with George Washington's citizen soldiers, in a democratic society not only the powerful count, so does each active citizen. Nowadays, New Jersey is a state, studded with Revolutionary War battlefields, that suffers from yawning voter apathy. Yet many of the state's eight million residents are intensely active in civic affairs. Volunteer fire departments, ambulance squads, garden clubs, environmental cleanups, youth sports teams, literacy volunteers, library associations, historic societies, student-exchange hosts, church and temple social action committees, and fund-raising drives for a multitude of causes abound in Garden State communities, as they do across America.

Grassroots actions of various sorts in New Jersey have helped spark national trends. This is a state that incubates innovative ideas—from Thomas Edison's illuminating inventions to finding good uses for garbage. Indeed, there is an exceedingly fine line in this compact state between volunteer, commercial, and government activity. A compelling idea developed in the state or borrowed from elsewhere often sparks interest among community activists, business people, and government officials. When innovators in the three sectors work together, the results can be astonishing.

For instance, in the 1970s and 1980s residents of several New Jersey towns launched garbage recycling projects that convinced their neighbors to bundle old newspapers, wash and bag glass bottles and tin cans, and help create community recycling programs that became state and national models. After initially rejecting the idea and its advocates, many municipal governments embraced recycling when it was demonstrated to them that they could get substantial amounts of cash for aluminum soda cans and other recyclables to offset increasingly expensive trash-hauling contracts. Becoming state policy in 1987, recycling salvaged 60 percent of New Jersey's household trash within a decade—greatly reducing the spread of the sprawling garbage dumps the state was infamous for, saving innumerable wetlands from being filled with household trash, cutting taxes by reducing garbage-hauling costs, and launching a multimillion-dollar recycling industry. In rural West Milford, high school students took this idea a step further, convincing the McDonald's restaurant chain to switch from throwaway packaging to recyclables, starting with the local fast-food franchise and expanding across the country. In the mundane, yet paradoxically popular, arena of recycling, volunteers in New Jersey changed government policy and business practices by mobilizing their friends and neighbors to do something together for the good of the community, the state, and the environment.

Despite this compelling example, a lot of people in New Jersey and across America sit on the sidelines on many other issues. "APATHY!" protested a crudely painted piece of graffiti facing a jam-packed North Jersey commuter highway in the economically comfy mid-1990s. Besides the utter non-involvement of apathy, people may not be active in the latest heated issue for another reason: volunteer fatigue—or, at least, uneasiness about taking on another cause. By one estimate, half of the population of the United States volunteers regularly for some activity, ranging from coaching kids' sports teams to typing a church bulletin, visiting hospital patients to collecting donations for UNICEF. As a protest sign held up outside the Presidents' Summit on Volunteerism in Philadelphia in 1997 put it, "We've volunteered enough to know volunteering is not enough." The protesters were targeting cutbacks in federal funding for social programs. The statement could also be read as a reflection on the fact that many volunteers feel that, despite their efforts, little or nothing tangible has been accomplished to resolve chronic social problems.

Hoping to make a difference, many people engage in several volunteer activities. Such efforts often leave people feeling spread too thin. Consider what a founder of an activist group called Minority Athletes Networking (MAN) has said about the frustrations of volunteering for many good causes. "Before MAN, I was on at least 10 different volunteer boards. I was putting a lot of blood and sweat into each. But I didn't feel I was making a difference," Ron Johnson, a former New York Giants football player, told a *Bergen Record* columnist. Johnson found that he felt more effective when he focused his energies, with those of other retired professional athletes, on a project to raise funds and help troubled inner-city youths attend college or get work-skills training. Focused on this goal, the Teaneck-based group helped set up a nonprofit window-blind factory in Paterson to provide employment training and a mentoring program for its members to provide advice, encouragement, and career counseling to youngsters flirting with dropping out of school. In five years, its two dozen or so members raised more than $170,000 for college scholarships through fund-raising banquets and other events. Its members take their high-energy educational recruiting mission into rough places such as a juvenile detention center in rural Ringwood, where one sixteen-year-old gave this testimonial: "Before they came, I felt like I was going down the drain. But they put a lot of stuff in my head, like hanging around with the right people as opposed to negative people. And making my goals reachable. I'm going to take heed in that."

Because it can be fit into busy lives, volunteering a little here and a little there seems more manageable than launching a new campaign. It is easier to volunteer a few hours in an established program that somebody else runs, and quite a different matter to organize a fresh civic campaign. The difference, however, can be not only feeling more effective, but being more effective. Focusing one's time and energy with a like-minded group of people on one project can produce tangible results—depending on the issue and the participants' skills and persistence. Even a campaign that ultimately is not successful may provide a seedbed of experience and ideas that were tried out in the crucible of public affairs for one that later does succeed.

"How can I find the time?" most busy people are likely to groan. If something is really important, people find the time, learning to juggle the elements of their lives better. One time-saving solution may be to drop some volunteer work to concentrate on a specific project. A civic or religious group you are active with may be willing to embrace the new campaign, if you make a good case for doing it. That's often the first step of organizing a project—convincing some activists you know to help launch a focused campaign. In many cases, however, people find there is little interest even among activists in addressing a particular problem, until somebody—maybe you—launches a campaign and makes a convincing case for why others should support it.

Unfortunately, civic action doesn't come with a user's manual. In response to growing interest in citizen activism, a number of how-to books on environmental, health, and other quality of life concerns have been published. Most are geared toward what an individual can do. That's a good start. But few works on citizen action, astonishingly, focus on how to work in concert with others to create a sustained campaign. Effective citizen campaigns don't just happen. They are carefully organized, passionately conducted, and persistently sustained. Their hard-won lessons, however, are seldom taught in civics classes or television programs. History books and television documentaries highlight the exploits of prominent individuals as the embodiment of social campaigns; they seldom show how numerous people work in concert with others to create a sustained grassroots campaign, usually without a celebrity in sight. News media coverage of protest marches and campaign rallies zeros in on the razzle-dazzle and sound bites by media-savvy participants, with scant examination of the depths of day-by-day activities that transform a cause into a cultural imperative.

This book presents the inside story of civic campaigns that worked. It is designed to be put to work—to provide an owners' manual for citizens, a handbook on civic action, a guidebook for creative improvements on the American dream. It celebrates the accomplishments of ordinary people who march, meet, write, petition, roll up their sleeves and effectively do something with their passion for peace, justice, human rights, environmental protection, historic preservation, improved quality of life, or a community-improvement project. Based on interviews with seasoned activists and my observations as a community news reporter and an organizer of peace campaigns at the community to international levels, here's the lively essence of grassroots citizen action that hopefully makes a difference in people's lives.

The case histories featured here provide memorable examples of citizens in action, organizing campaigns with clear-cut goals whose accomplishments can be measured. They show the process of putting together progressively more complex civic projects. The focus is on the work of organizing, rather than that of being a volunteer for a good cause. Millions of Americans have been volunteers; far fewer have learned to be organizers of volunteers. One reason is that there's no national academy for citizen activists equivalent to America's military academies and university graduate schools for various professions. Another reason is that activist organizations offer a confusing smorgasbord of organizing training, often narrowly focused by ideological blinders. Peace groups, for instance, traditionally have focused on protest marches, civil disobedience, and vigils to demonstrate moral witness. It is hard to teach people how to change government policies when government has been demonized in emotionally heated demonstrations as the enemy. Pro-life and pro-choice groups have turned the abortion issue into a religious battlefield with no compromise allowed between absolute positions. When people are shouted at to choose sides, what is being promoted is not democracy. Too many activist groups teach by their actions and words that the bottom line in civic affairs is raw power—and the side that can mobilize the most power wins. That's what lots of people have learned from the way politics is conducted in America. Citizen groups that follow that path, however, generally fail to command much allegiance from the public. And without widespread public support, such campaigns generally fail. Think about it: would you devote yourself as a volunteer in a civic campaign because someone pressured you to do it?

Volunteerism is the bedrock of civic action. That's what distinguishes it from government operations. Volunteers do it because they choose to. While I'm critical of the conduct of many citizen campaigns, I doubt that any government could teach civic activism. Government agencies and elected officials have a habit of operating on behalf of the public in as much secrecy as can be gotten away with, then ordering citizens to accept the resulting policies. That doesn't teach citizenship. It treats voters and taxpayers as foot soldiers. The essence of democracy, to me, is that the citizens, not a back room full of bureaucrats, decide. And citizens can't make good decisions without a full airing of issues and full disclosure of the known facts and options.

The best school for democracy is a citizens' group that

researches the issue it is concerned about, educates its members and the public about the issue and proposed solutions, and treats other activist groups, the public, government officials, and people on the other side of the issue as fellow human beings, asked to bridge their differences for the common good. These are groups that invoke the appeal of common sense developed through the civic process of public debate and discussion. Outgunned in traditional arenas of power, they create new arenas by demonstrating better ideas than what governments, politicians, and self-serving special interests propose. And they find that people have a tremendous capacity for working cooperatively when asked to assist a campaign whose demonstrable aim is the common good of a neighborhood, region, nation, or the world.

"Nonprofits . . . have this wonderful way of tapping individual initiative, but they do it for public purposes," notes Lester M. Salamon, coauthor of a 1998 Johns Hopkins University report on civic organizations. Salamon's study of nonprofit activities in the United States, Europe, Israel, Japan, and Latin America found a $1.1 trillion social action industry that employs more people than the largest private corporations do and attracts an "average of 28 percent of the population" as volunteers. The major sources of income for such civic activities are contributions from the public and fees for services, with grants from foundations and corporations providing a little over 10 percent, the study found. "Such institutions can give expression to citizen concerns, hold governments accountable, promote community, address unmet needs, and generally improve the quality of life," the Johns Hopkins study concluded.

Lots of people have learned what determined citizens can do in campaigns of all sorts. They don't wear campaign medals, but they've taken on issues and forces that soldiers have feared to tackle. Citizen action doesn't command armies. It mobilizes ordinary folks, however, to do extraordinary things. Veterans of such campaigns have something richer than war stories to share.

Some Americans don Revolutionary War costumes and reenact famous battles and encampments. That kind of activity offers participants and spectators a sense of what life was like for the nation's founders. Waging a citizen campaign not only re-creates that heritage but also makes new history. Participants are actors in the real workings of a civic movement, wrestling with a crucial current issue. They share the sensations that Thomas Paine's generation must have felt in creating the world's first nation with elected leaders and a citizen's Bill of Rights. That revolutionary grassroots movement established the principle that social action rightfully is a civic activity, not a monopoly of monarchs. Pioneering citizen activists such as William Penn and Benjamin Franklin, followed by Elizabeth Cady Stanton, Jane Addams, and many others, created and spread the barn-raising ethic of the American frontier, of neighbors getting together and forming a civic group to tackle a common problem without waiting for a nod of government approval.

"Americans of all ages, all conditions, and all dispositions constantly form associations. . . . Wherever at the head of some new undertaking you see the government in France, or a man of rank in England, in the United States you will be sure to find an association. . . . I have often admired the extreme skill with which the inhabitants of the United States succeed in proposing a common object for the exertions of a great many men and inducing them voluntarily to pursue it," Alexis de Tocqueville wrote in *Democracy in America*, that landmark study of life in the young United States. The French visitor was fascinated by the fact that ordinary Americans constantly formed civic groups to address issues that in Europe were reserved for the ruling class.

"We do not take our cue as Americans from the White House or from Congress. They take their cue from us," stated Charles Kuralt, another widely traveled observer of the American scene, a century and a half after Tocqueville. From his *On the Road* television reports, Kuralt was impressed by the hardy spirit of grassroots activism thriving in communities across the country. "All through the so-called selfish eighties, so many people were working at addressing problems," he told a packed auditorium at William Paterson College in a talk on the state of America in November 1990. "The impulses for humaneness and justice are actually stronger than they used to be. It's happening outside of Washington—in some cases, despite Washington. . . . I'm impressed by those people who just take the job on themselves," Kuralt said. In more than thirty years as a television reporter, he saw America come a "good long way," he continued, thanks to citizens who got together and took up a cause. That kind of activism, he said, had grown over the years to include many unsung Americans. "They have become kind of the rule rather than the exception," Kuralt concluded.

Still, how often have you heard: *"Nothing can be done. Don't rock the boat. Nobody listens to us little people."* Despite this seemingly widespread apathetic attitude, modern America was shaped by the civil rights, consumer, environmental, and women's rights movements—campaigns that enlisted millions of Americans. The changes wrought by these campaigns were not created by presidential proclamations. They were the result of a national accumulation of small group actions that changed attitudes, which changed our culture and amended our laws.

That's not to say that social change—or preservation of a natural or historic site or community quality of life—is easy to accomplish, given the weight of tradition on one hand, and the profit-driven pressures of "progress" on the other. Seeking a solution through the ballot box is an ordeal. In many elections, most voters don't vote. Serious discussion of social issues is lost in the shouting on talk shows and at news media circus events. Candidates for public office ignore, or waffle on, the concerns of ordinary folks. That's the familiar downside of democracy. The saving grace of American life is that citizens don't have to wait for politicians to act. In innumerable ways, this is a do-it-yourself democracy.

Citizen action is tough work, however. Think of starting a new business. Some people find they have a knack for launching and running a thriving business venture. Likewise, some find they have a knack for organizing people around a cause and become dynamic "social entrepreneurs." Most new businesses in America fail, however. Civic enterprises also flounder. Movements often rise in righteous wrath but lose steam and deflate when they cannot sustain a long-term campaign. The dismal reality is that many civic campaigns fizzle. They fail, in many cases, because they run out of creative ideas and energy. Sometimes they fail because the public rejects, or declines to support, the campaign's goal or leadership. That's one of the vital but little discussed "checks and balances" of democracy. Clashing "factions" of citizens, as the framers of the U.S. Constitution called them, need to muster widespread public support to advance their cause over that of opponents. That's the acid test of civic leadership in American society. Campaigns often fail because organizers are impatient and unwilling to expend the effort to build support among their fellow citizens.

Too often, activists blame an apathetic public when a campaign stalls. But the fault lines of human frailty, as Shakespeare noted, lie within. After writing letters to officials, attending meetings, holding rallies and marches, and voting, many activists often don't know what else to do when nothing changes—or when they win the first round. Sustaining a civic campaign for more than a season, in many cases for years, is one of the most trying experiences in life. The key factors in effective campaigns are not arcane mysteries: they include a clear goal, dedicated participants, a well-designed strategy of action, public outreach, creative responses to counterattacks and other obstacles, perseverance—and good timing. The hardest part is knowing how to put it all together.

Those who take up a good cause often expend too much effort in reinventing the wheel of civic action. Learning what works can be difficult. The process of civic problem solving does not attract television specials or talk show discussion. It takes patience to convey it and patience to learn it. How it works is not easily divined from books. Like learning to ride a bicycle, it takes doing. The best teachers are veterans of successful civic campaigns. But these busy people often burn out, retire, or move on to deal with long-delayed family or career matters, their hard-won expertise lost to others. Some civic projects leave a bitter taste, particularly if a campaign fails or participants are treated in a roughshod way by fellow activists. You may run into bitter survivors of past campaigns. They can be discouraging. Yet, if you're willing to listen, they may give sound advice on pitfalls to avoid. If you're cheerfully persistent in advancing your cause, they may lend you a hand. Respect snappish veterans: they speak from experience. Successful civic campaigns learn from and in many cases grow out of, but in any case transcend, previous campaigns.

One of the bitterest experiences for many Americans was that now-mythic era of activism, the 1960s. It's hard to glean useful lessons from a time of divisive social battles that a generation of aging adults still finds hard to discuss dispassionately. It was a time when protesters and protectors of the establishment shouted at each other, rather than listening and seeking common ground. Civic action, however, need not be conducted like a grim avenging angel swooping down on political miscreants. Especially at the community level, a civic campaign can be waged with gusto. It can be a thoroughly enjoyable, even exhilarating interaction with a wide range of people one might otherwise never meet. It can enrich your life, as well as that of others.

"Citizen organizing . . . transforms people's lives," note the authors of a 1970s tribute to grassroots activism, *Citizen Action and the New American Populism*. "It brings out the collective power that they have to change events large and small. It creates a collective voice for those who would otherwise go unheard. It teaches people that they can confront those who are highly placed, better educated, more powerful, or richer than themselves and win. It confirms things that people knew in their hearts to be right, although the 'experts' tried to convince them that they were wrong. . . . Through organization, people learn alternatives to lives of quiet desperation . . . They learn the skills of writing, speaking, managing large enterprises . . . through organizing, ordinary people come to possess the skills and abilities that those with [elite] education or wealth have always taken for granted."

That's a succinct description of the personal benefits of participating in a citizen campaign. However, as the tone indicates, it was written by veterans of sixties activism who viewed the situation through a leftist lens of class warfare. In reality, unlike union strikes and revolutions, effective civic campaigns bridge social and economic classes, bringing together rich and poor, the middle class and the working class, Democrats and Republicans, anarchists and socialists, college-educated professionals and high school dropouts. A civic campaign in Newark, for instance, that defeated government plans to locate a toxic waste incinerator next to a residential neighborhood "spurred many to reach across racial lines, cultures and generations," the *Star-Ledger* reported in a feature on the Ironbound section that a headline writer dubbed "activists' turf." Besides neighborhood residents, the Ironbound Committee Against Toxic Waste also organized suburbanites to aid the campaign, a common strategy in New Jersey, where many suburban residents grew up or attended college in cities or work in one and often stay involved with urban issues.

Joining with fellow citizens in a good cause can be a revitalizing experience, a highlight of one's life. It can also be frightening. Much depends on how well one learns to cope with the raw side of public affairs, including the mudslinging of "dirty politics." Engaging in citizen action may mean facing fears of speaking in public, of becoming an object of ridicule, or worse. *Gadfly. Communist. Socialist. Agitator.* These are just some of the names civic activists have been called by other Americans. Similar fulminations were directed at women who wanted the right to vote, people who opposed slavery, the revolutionaries who created the United States of America. Some people just can't stand to see other people enjoying the same rights they reserve for themselves. Engaging in citizen action puts people face to face with the often nasty side of public life. The gap between textbook descriptions of democracy and the way things actually work is disconcerting. Character assassination, threats, intimidation, and other slimy forms of gutter politics are often wielded against citizen activists. It is a bruising, intense struggle to confront powerful forces defending the status quo or pressing their vision of progress. The gritty reality is that democracy as practiced by many participants is a knock-down, drag-out fight among wrangling partisans passionately committed to incompatible interests. To reverse Clauswitz's infamous military dictum, politics for many is war by other means.

The best weapons a civic activist can have—weapons that confound the wannabe warriors—are insistence on nonviolent means to a nonviolent end, a spirit that rises to stiff challenges, a straightforward agenda, and a good sense of humor. Skills one may need to acquire, or sharpen, include conflict resolution, diplomacy, public speaking, time management, and public safety. (If you call a protest rally or public meeting, you have a responsibility for the safety of participants.) Depending on what you decide to focus on doing in a civic campaign, you should also master writing news releases and other forms of publicity, press interviews, fund-raising, bookkeeping, research, letter writing, envelope stuffing, moderating meetings, lobbying, networking, volunteer coordination and training, and strategic planning. Those are the basic skills a citizens' campaign needs to deploy. Technical skills may be needed as well—how to produce a newsletter and use computers, video cameras, slide projectors, and other tools. Since one person can't possibly do all these things, other key skills are recruitment, delegation of responsibilities, and coordination of multiple activities by many people.

Not least, a citizens' campaign needs to develop self-confidence among its members in their collective vision. Among the first hurdles citizen activists have to face are the cruel retorts that are flung at civic campaigns, warning of insurmountable barriers. "You can't fight City Hall" has become a modern American maxim. You bet you can fight City Hall. People do it all the time—and change the programs, priorities, and occupants of government offices. But "City Hall" may be the least of a citizen campaign's hurdles.

City Hall may become an ally, if a good networking job is done. There may be far more formidable barriers and pitfalls for people launching a civic campaign, including sharp elbows from competing activists and hard knocks from defenders of the status quo or promoters of self-serving development.

Astute politicians jump aboard the bandwagon of a popular cause. But they wait for somebody else to organize it, while gauging public opinion. When politicians embrace a cause, they bring media attention to it. They may also try to fold a popular citizen campaign into their political campaigning, which can undermine its public appeal. To counter this takes diplomacy and a firm stand that this is a bipartisan civic campaign. Government workers also test the cultural winds. Often, many will assist a project that has popular appeal. Government employees, after all, are also citizens and like to feel involved in memorable public events. Some bureaucrats may offer only sabotage, however; in that case, someone else in government may decide to counter that and assist the campaign, perhaps to spite the spiteful official.

A substantial roadblock can be expected to be raised by defenders of the status quo or vested interests, who may have great influence in government circles. Yet, if engaged forthrightly on the plane of public debate, staunch opponents help heighten interest in an issue. A campaign that generates widespread support as being in the public interest may see the opposition melt away. Powerful special interests, the kind that throw their weight around government agencies, generally prefer a backroom deal to the glare of public debate.

Just as a civic campaign seems poised for success, another roadblock can pop up—set by other activists, protective of what they see as their turf, seeking to swing support for a new campaign into their camp. Successful civic campaigns must outmaneuver fierce opposition, fraternal infighting, and political co-optation. They do this by building a widespread grassroots network focused on public education and action that average citizens can support through voting in a referendum or by working as campaign activists, letter writers, and financial contributors. Effective civic organizers set a clearly focused agenda, foster supportive public opinion, welcome volunteers, gain the support or begrudging respect of government officials, sidestep grudge matches with opponents and other activists, and follow through to accomplish a clearly stated goal. One measure of effectiveness is that well-organized civic actions challenge the attitude of "that's the way things are." They make waves and they make things happen. They say: "Let's do it!"—and get it done.

At the center of such campaigns is a core of people committed to a cause they believe is for the public good and are willing to take to the public, rolling up their sleeves and doing a lot of spadework, providing civic leadership by example. "There are figureheads, and then there are workers," observed Stephanie Zonenberg, a community activist in the hardscrabble city of Paterson. What she calls "the consistent, persistent people" get things done—such as reclaiming a park in her city that had been taken over by drug dealers, transforming a trash-strewn shooting gallery back into a community garden spot. "The real heroes," said Zonenberg, "are those quiet people who make the community work."

Such heroes generally find they can't do it alone. Many campaigns are sustained by one person's persistence, which inspires others. Sometimes a community improvement project, such as planting flowers, can be done by one person. If you can handle alone what you're concerned about, you don't need this book. Some people like to work alone, yet lend their efforts to a larger cause. They should not be discouraged from participating in a larger project. There are many ways to be engaged in a civic campaign. By its nature, a large enterprise requires cooperation and coordination for a common goal. Participants can play many roles—working alone, in small groups, in coalitions. Meshing a diverse collection of people into a focused civic campaign takes a particular brand of leadership.

"A lot of people spend a lot of wasted time at meetings talking," said Stephanie Zonenberg, who prefers action to talk. She admires community activists who "see a job that needs to be done and do it." On the other hand, she realizes that some people have to attend meetings to set the direction of a campaign. In her neighborhood of 1,200 homes, about 120 families are members of the community association that tackled cleaning up the neighborhood park. Far fewer attend meetings. Most prefer to get their information about upcoming events and what needs to be done from the group's newsletter. "We've had very good leadership," Zonenberg said of the persistent little group that meets on a regular basis to direct the park cleanup and preservation campaign. "We've had very good people along the way that focused it."

The key to every effective citizens' campaign is focusing a lot of individual efforts on a common goal. That takes articulate talkers, who can frame the issue and convey proposed solutions, as well as dedicated doers. For campaigns seeking to change ingrained public attitudes that foster apathy and self-help groups seeking to transform stereotypes about areas of the human condition painful for people to deal with, focused talk is perhaps the paramount action. Civic campaigns, in contrast to military and political campaigns, are mounted by people concerned about the health of their community and its environment, ranging from their backyard to the planet Earth. Some civic campaigns address external problems, some address internal problems—that is, crises inside people. Whatever its focus, virtually every citizen campaign must start out by describing the problem in a compelling way to other people busy with their own lives, then make a convincing case that collective action can foster a sensible solution.

Talking and writing done as outreach to others are vital components of any civic campaign. Written and verbal communication—via letters, newsletters, letters-to-editors, organizational meetings, public forums, private discussions—focused on building support for a citizens' campaign creates a collective effort, called networking. "Networking has often led to the early identification of new or growing health or social problems, as people began to recognize their similarities, and come together to form self-help groups. . . . Indeed, the seeds of many long-standing health foundations, societies, and agencies dealing with various health and social problems have historically first taken the form of mutual aid self-help groups or networks," says Edward J. Madara, the founder and director of the New Jersey Self-Help Clearinghouse and the American Self-Help Clearinghouse, both located at Saint Clare's Health Services in Denville. Madara's statewide and national clearinghouses provide listings for more than four thousand self-help groups in New Jersey and more than eight hundred in other states.

Whether addressing the problems of people with rare diseases or public policy on epidemics such as AIDS, mutual-help groups formed by the afflicted and the affected who become activists rely on the power of their voices to raise the issues and propose solutions. Addressing the health of a neighborhood, the natural environment, or international affairs is akin to tackling an internal disorder. The best medicine is taking action to mobilize people's talents and energies to find and effect a remedy or a way of alleviating the suffering of a chronic condition.

Neighborhoods rise and fall depending on the level of civic activism. Wilderness is paved or saved depending on the level of citizen action. Nations wage or prevent war depending on the level of citizen interaction. People suffering painful personal turmoil survive or die depending on the level and quality of interaction with other people. The antidote to apathy or despair is doing something positive about something that blights our life, community, or world. This is a healing process for human bodies and the body politic that is beyond politics or medicine. This is communion in action. This is the high of barn raising. A civic campaign in full flower is an emotionally exciting, spiritual experience. One feels good doing good with others. This is no "pie in the sky" stuff, but the down-to-earth result of a well-organized and focused civic campaign. It is memorable real-life drama.

Like dramas on stage and screen, civic campaigns thrive when they have good directors. They falter under poor direction. To a great degree, citizen activists learn by trial and error, discovering the complexities of organizing fellow humans in the process of trying to transform apathetic, otherwise busy, or polarized communities and via encounters with often brusque veteran organizers who've "been there, done that." Finding workable models can be hard. The military model—barking orders—backfires with civilian volunteers. The business firm model—assigning tasks to be done or else get fired—doesn't work well with people volunteering their own free time. The political campaign model, which often consists of opponents ducking issues while jabbing each other, has a lot of shortcomings, one of which is that it's not aimed at solving problems. A civic campaign challenges people to set aside their differences and work together for a common purpose. It operates on a very different set of dynamics—cooperation and mutual assistance—than people have experienced in the competitive arenas of American society. It combines elements of ecumenical religious appeals with the self-discipline, goal-oriented focus, and teamwork of mountain climbers. It is a *campaign*! It focuses enormous amounts of energy and passion. Fully engaged, it generates a magnetism that attracts people—or repels them.

That magnetism can work wonders, bending even governments to respect the goal of a citizens' campaign. That outcome, however, generally requires the timely assistance of supportive officials. They are the indispensable allies of citizen groups. They know how government works. They often got their start in public affairs as civic activists. But they seldom get as much attention for their mediating style of governing as the news media gives to the flamboyance of autocrats. They are often in the minority in the arena of power, where competing deal makers advance monied special interests. They can accomplish little for the public good without the support of an aroused citizens' campaign.

"I often tell people: Don't let me carry your banner," said the wily head of a city agency. "You carry your banner. You'll have more success than I will. You go to the council meeting. Let the council tell me to do this. That's how it works. Don't give me your ideas and let me go down there. You go down there and let them tell me: 'We like this idea, get it going.'"

Enough said about the joys, pitfalls, and complexities of citizen action. You want to do something! You want to make a difference on an issue that's of great concern to you and perhaps many other people. What you need is an effective way to organize people who agree on this matter and

transform grassroots concerns into concrete accomplishment. Besides dynamic tactics and strategy, a successful citizens' campaign thrives on inspirational examples. The most
compelling attraction of a civic campaign, and the greatest
aid for organizers, is knowing it can be done. Read on.

2

Rebuilding

Urban

Neighborhoods,

Lot by Lot

[We're] part of the American spirit—jump in and
fix it. The people do it themselves.
—Barbara Dunn, Paterson Habitat for Humanity

You can't get much more grassroots than
a neighborhood park. One of the most satisfying civic actions is the transformation of a neighborhood eyesore into
an object of community pride. For one community, the eyesore was a weather-beaten, graffiti-sprayed playground. This
was sacrilege to the neighborhood of tidy homes and
trimmed lawns. Its hardworking taxpayers expected the city
to fix it. A department of public works crew dutifully
painted over the offensive scribbles with mismatched
splotches of paint, which were rehit by swirls of graffiti.
Adults fumed. Watching his young daughter swinging in
the playground one day, a father had an idea: What if the

ugly old place was turned into something so beautiful no one would dare deface it?

ABCs of a Cleanup Campaign

What began as one man's idea became a campaign. Surrounded by chain-link fences, the children's playground in Clifton's Lakeview Park lies in the shadow of the DPW garage and traffic streams on the Garden State Parkway. The predominant hue of the battered swings, slide, seesaws, and benches was a dull brownish green slapped over layers of other colors that peeked through scratches. The freshest paint was black swirls of crude graffiti. All this offended Greg Baron, a piano tuner by trade, who felt his daughter and other neighborhood children deserved better. Baron set about enlisting volunteers to repaint the playground. His daughter and other kids designed cartoon characters, leaf motifs, and educational themes. Among the volunteer painting crew were convicted graffiti vandals. Such a combination of elements enticed a newspaper editor to assign a photographer and reporter to cover this colorful community event. For jaded journalists, this was a change from daily urban crime bulletins.

Shortly after the unorthodox painting party got underway, a group of teenagers from neighboring Paterson sauntered into the playground. Suspicions were high in the Clifton neighborhood that Paterson kids had painted the graffiti. After making a reconnaissance to check out what was going on, a lookout shouted to his friends. In a clump of sneakers and baggy blue jeans, the sullen boys slouched over to inspect what had been a dingy bench. The metal back now boasted a gleaming row of enormous ABC blocks in bright primary colors perched above a five-foot-long yellow-and-black ruler painted on the seat. Voicing the group vibes, one of the teens issued this terse pronouncement: "It's good. Kids could play and learn at the same time."

A city official who had provided sixty dollars from the parks department budget to buy several boxes of spray-can paint stopped by and beamed with approval at the bright streaks and swoops being applied to rusted, graffiti-marred surfaces. "It's a people project," a recreation commissioner said of the volunteer work. "Looks good!" a leader of the neighborhood civic association told the painters. "I love it—what I can do with a can of spray paint," said Joe, a Paterson high school student whose blatant tagging had landed him in jail, as he carefully retouched alphabet letters on a bench. Deftly switching paint cans and retouching another color block, Joe said he was glad to volunteer when he heard some people in Clifton were looking for help on a park project. "Graffiti is an art," he said. "It's not meant for vandalism."

Two years later, the playground was still unmarred by graffiti. Some shiny new playground equipment had been provided by a penny-pinching city council. Using the experience gained in revitalizing the playground, Baron and other members of the Lakeview Civic Association shifted their sights, organizing painting parties of community groups to transform graffiti-sprayed highway underpasses into artistic showcases featuring swirling leaves, wheeling doves, tropical fish, and galloping herds of horses.

"Make it fun, and people will join you," Baron said when asked what lessons he learned from the playground project. "Art has more power than just plain paint. The [vandals] don't want to mess with good art," he said. Other tactics Baron employed included inviting suggestions of what to paint from kids who play in the park and from kids whose previous idea of what to do with a can of paint was a graffiti spree. Baron searched out graffiti sprayers in Paterson and asked them how they would spiff up a playground. "The

kids, they set the pace. These were street punks, is the way
we think of them. They set the pace for an educational thing,
which was colorful and fun. My daughter and other kids got
involved, including a kid who lives in the neighborhood and
now looks out for that playground. It was that DPW mus-
tard green, with sexual and racial graffiti all over it," Baron
said of the urban-jumble canvas they started with. "We just
added color, and bam! Everybody came. I learned this from
graffiti artists. They showed me how to defeat graffiti"—by
displaying eye-catching artistry that trumps graffiti taggers'
contemptuous comment on urban blight.

The playground project helped spur a citywide campaign
by civic groups to clean up graffiti. It also helped a coalition
of parents get funds from the city council to replace out-
moded playground equipment. "The painting of the park
wasn't traditional, but it worked out very well," said Dawn
Kaiser, president of the Lakeview Civic Association. "That
project drew a lot of attention to the [condition of the] parks.
If you compare Clifton to the way it was a few years ago, we
really cleaned up a lot." The key to a successful community project, she said, is building enthusiasm among a few
people, as Greg Baron did. That attracts others to get involved. Ask people to help solve a specific problem, said
Kaiser. "And a lot of times, you can surprise yourself with
what can be done."

"Flower Power" Project

In neighboring Paterson, once-fashionable Eastside
Park was so blighted it frightened away adults. "It was over-
run with prostitutes, drug dealers. Women, children, old
people were afraid to venture into the park," Stephanie
Zonenberg said of the centerpiece of her stately residential
neighborhood. While homeowners zealously maintained

their private plots, the neglected public park had become one of the city's most dangerous areas. Determined neighbors found a solution: mobilize volunteers to clean up litter and graffiti, plant flowers, and lay down the rules to rambunctious youngsters. Now, where condoms and beer cans used to litter the ground, families and school groups play and tend flower and vegetable gardens.

"One spring day, when there was gridlock in the park, with people playing loud boom boxes, and doing their deals with drugs, drinking, and littering, and making a mess out of our park, we called the police. They told us it was just too dangerous for them to go into the park," Zonenberg recalled. "So we said: 'It's our park, so we'll do something.' What we did is, we went around to each automobile, each group of kids, and said to them: 'We are the neighbors here. We want you to use the park. It's a beautiful park. It's fine that you come. We want you to come. But there's rules listed in the park. You might not have noticed. The rules say: No loud music, no abusive language, no alcohol, no drugs, and your dogs must be on leashes. And no littering.' And they looked at us and they said: 'Why'd you let us get away with it for so long?' We chatted with them for a while, and they came up with the idea that next week they were going to have a rally. No drugs, no alcohol, no litter. The kids. They got permits from the city council and the next week they had that rally. That was back in 1990. Now for seven years, each year they've had what they call an Afro-American Day. It's very, very nice. A parade comes up Broadway. They come into the park. They spend the day. The next day you wouldn't know. There's no bottles of alcohol around, there's no litter."

That solution, however, only worked for some park visitors. Others still came to do drugs, spray graffiti on marble seats and statues, and litter the landscape with booze bottles,

soda cans, and whatever else they wanted to discard. Muggers sometimes lurked in the bushes. Neighborhood residents were split over what to do about the hard-core
characters who refused to reform their behavior. "There was
another group that just laughed at us," Zonenberg said of
some cynics. "They went into this whole thing to fight
crime. They got vests, they got these bullhorns, and they
got a system of patrol. And we said, 'no—we're going to do
a different way. We're going to pick up litter,'" she laughed.
"'We're going to plant flowers.' And they laughed at us. Their
group has now disintegrated. But we're still going."

To foil muggers, volunteers trimmed bushes to eliminate hiding places. To counter graffiti, neighbors scrubbed
it off as quickly as it appeared. To discourage littering, several neighbors patrolled the park and picked up litter daily.
To encourage community use of the park, residents organized festive events, planted flowers, and cleared an over-
grown hillside to create a "Friendship Garden" of mixed
flowers and vegetables. School groups, senior citizens, and
numerous other city residents with green thumbs and a sense
of adventure dropped by to help in the garden. With so much
community-spirited activity going on and so many potential witnesses to nasty behavior, antisocial types drifted elsewhere. City officials took notice. Funds were found to restore
a deteriorating Victorian house that had once been a centerpiece of the park.

"We continued through that summer to clean up the
park, not with police power, which was useless, but with
flower power, we called it," said Zonenberg, a housewife
determined to raise four children in a rough-and-tumble city.
"The citizen patrols are the people that do the gardening.
It's not very threatening. When you meet someone gardening, you start chitchatting. . . . We had barbecues, we had
family picnics, we had gospel songfests, we had karate dem-

onstrations, we had cleanup days. And that's what we've continued, since 1990. I think it's empowered the people. Previous to that time, you would hear at community meetings: 'The Public Works Department doesn't do their job. The policemen don't do their job. We still have this problem of noise, drugs.' But, once we took responsibility, that's what changed it all," she said of the park restoration project undertaken by members of the Eastside Neighborhood Association. "Volunteerism turned around the neighborhood. It makes a lot of difference. It puts pride back into people. The garden is a demonstration that people can come out and work together and they can change the conditions of their community. Now, with all these volunteers, it makes everyone feel a lot safer. We've changed it," Zonenberg said of the park's transformation. "I think we could be a model for the whole country."

Building Houses and Neighborhoods

One of the most sophisticated grassroots campaigns these days transforms litter-strewn lots into new homes and renewed neighborhoods. In a modern version of frontier barn raising, volunteer work crews for Habitat for Humanity projects are building houses for low-income people in communities across the United States and internationally. It is an idea that grew from a seed sown in Georgia, where a visionary group of Christians decided to put their beliefs about brotherhood into practice, erecting sturdy houses to replace tenant farmers' shacks. With missionary zeal, that idea of neighbors lending a hand to help less fortunate neighbors build a decent home of their own was spread to many other parts of the country and the world. When it arrived in New Jersey in the early 1980s, it was a radical concept. Would it work in cities torn by race riots, white flight to

the suburbs, and multimillion-dollar government urban re-
newal projects that had spectacularly failed to improve
blighted blocks?

How could a citizens' campaign succeed where the federal government's War on Poverty had failed? "We started
with just a handful—five of us, really. And the five of us got
people that we knew and brought them in, and they got
people they knew and brought them in," recalled Ed Smith,
a suburban Bergen County resident who was recruited to
help build houses in a dismal part of Paterson by a minister
who knew Smith was a carpenter. First one house was built
by volunteers and the family that would live there. And
then another one, and another one. Then a whole block of
townhouses—twenty-eight in all, in a new development
called Habitat Way—was built on the site of a burnt-out
warehouse. In 1998, Smith oversaw the simultaneous construction of ten homes built by hundreds of volunteers
at several locations in what had been a virtually abandoned
section of the city called Northside, bringing to eighty-five
the number of houses built by Paterson Habitat for Humanity in a little over a decade.

"This was like a forgotten place; it was like a place that
had been totally erased off the map," James Staton, president of the Paterson Habitat Homeowners Association, told
a news reporter in 1995, when the local affiliate of Habitat
for Humanity was a recipient of *The Record*'s Community
Service Award. Added Bishop Joseph Robertson of the As-
sembly Holy House of Prayer, a neighborhood church: "The
Habitat project has given the whole area an uplift. Before,
you walked down the streets and you saw vacant lots and
weeds growing. Now, I see flowers and green bushes, and
children coming out of houses and going to school."

This is the story of how primarily white middle-class
suburbanites and minority working-class city residents

worked together to create a modern miracle. The section of the faded mill city this campaign tackled had not seen a new house built in decades. While shopping malls, industrial parks, corporate offices, and housing tracts mushroomed across the suburbs, Paterson's Northside was a bleak place of unkempt tenements, trash-strewn empty lots, and abandoned factories. Then along came a reform group hardly anyone had heard of before.

"When we got started, the hard part was to go out and tell the world who we were. It was really a tough job," said Tony Sinacore, a board member and past president of the group. "There were two ministers that really got it started—John Algera and Stan VanderKlay. They went from church to church to church and they spoke. And they got the Reformed churches involved and the Presbyterian churches involved, etc. Now, today we have five hundred to six hundred churches that support us. Now we have the corporations coming in" with volunteer work crews and financial donations as well as college students who trek to Paterson from several states, and even international volunteers.

Once launched, the visionary preachers of this grassroots project discovered that getting people to work together to build houses is a monumental task. "In the beginning, we had a lot of these volunteers who were ex-construction guys and they didn't want any part of these novice volunteers," said Sinacore. "We kept saying, 'Hey, the novice volunteers are our backbone—the guys who bring us the money and make our organization grow.' There was this constant battle. So we had to work with all these 'sophisticated' volunteers to convince them that they had to work with the nonskilled volunteers. It took a long time to get them to do that. But it finally did set in, because they realized they couldn't buy the materials if they didn't get the money and those nonskilled workers that showed up are the people who brought the checks. They finally recognized that it was important to work with those people who didn't know how to hammer a nail, and teach them how to hammer a nail—and they'll come back. They'll come back and bring their friends. And that's exactly what happened. They brought their friends, and their friends brought their friends, etc., etc. And we just grew! I believe that's the cornerstone that made it all happen: When all these people started to recognize that we're all in this for one reason, and that reason is to give a person a decent place to live. And we should put our pride and all our problems behind us, rather than argue over who's going to teach who and all that kind of stuff."

Sinacore, an electronic instruments engineer who lives in a suburban community, was recruited into the housing project by his wife, Mary, one of the founders. Both were attracted by the practicality of the Habitat plan: houses built by volunteer work crews and the people who would live there, sold at a price that just covers the cost of construction materials to low-income families through a zero-interest mortgage with low monthly payments. The mortgage payments are recycled back into the building fund to help finance more homes. "I was very interested in housing," said Mary Sinacore, a bookkeeper who was doing volunteer work in a Paterson church when she heard about the Habitat project. "It was like God answered a prayer. I would see these streets and feel that I wish I could go in there and renovate them. But how could I do this by myself? Then here was this proposal."

The idea for Habitat for Humanity grew out of home-building projects in rural Georgia and in Zaire that, in the 1970s, launched Millard and Linda Fuller on a visionary, yet practical religious mission, one that took the couple from an affluent business-oriented life in Montgomery, Alabama, to a nonprofit lifestyle organizing volunteers to spend hot, sweaty days in city lots and dusty fields hammering and sawing to build new or renovated houses for people struggling to keep a roof over their heads. The movement they and a couple dozen friends launched at Koinonia Farm on the outskirts of Americus, Georgia, in 1976 spread to every state and dozens of other countries. With former President Jimmy Carter and other celebrities joining thousands of people, housing has been built in numbers that boggle the mind: fifty thousand houses in twenty years, from Armenia to Zambia, Alaska to Florida; fifty-two new homes built in a week in seven rural Appalachian communities; one hundred homes erected in Houston in a work blitz led by Jimmy Carter; one thousand houses built in fifty villages near Mexico City. Paterson is not on the celebrity circuit. So its Habitat project began and maintained a slow, steady pace. Building lots were initially obtained by convincing the city council to donate empty lots acquired in tax foreclosures for one dollar each. When these were built on, the group bought more land through tax sales and negotiations with owners of burned or decayed buildings. The board of directors kept the momentum of volunteers and financial donations going by working to have at least one house-building project always underway. "It was just part of the wisdom of the people involved, because they knew that once you stop building, the money doesn't come in," Mary Sinacore said.

The Paterson group kept an eye on other Habitat projects and tried to learn from their mistakes. "There are over one thousand Habitats across the country, but not all of them are building. They have met various obstacles," she said. "Sometimes it's the board makeup. Sometimes the board spends more time disagreeing with how you should do something. Sometimes they have resistance from the community. Sometimes a community doesn't want to be known as a community that needs such a thing as Habitat. It's, like, an embarrassment. Sometimes the politicians have their own plans, that doesn't include a Habitat group. We did not have these problems in Paterson, so we were very blessed."

A headache arose for Paterson Habitat office volunteers handling mortgage payments, however. Getting many new homeowners to keep up monthly mortgage payments was a problem in Habitat projects across the country, which a 1997 Associated Press investigation lambasted. The problem was resolved in Paterson when a supporter at a bank offered free professional services. "Instead of people sending the money to the Habitat office, it gets sent to a bank," said Mary Sinacore. "If they're late three times, they get a letter that requires them to go to financial counseling. That's the same program the bank has for their customers. So that helps us, because people have a little more respect that they're sending it to a bank. When they were sending it to us, they would call with all kinds of excuses. When I was the treasurer, some homeowners would call me up in the middle of the night. The bank offered to do it as a free service. We have not had any foreclosures. We had one or two people that moved, but it was for other reasons. All the rest of the people are living in their home and paying their monthly payment. Bankers we talk with tell us that the record we have with our homeowners beats the record they have with their people who have mortgages."

Other problems that cropped up were solved by hiring professionals to handle work that volunteers found difficult to maintain year after year. "We've had some excellent site coordinators who have been very good with working with volunteers, showing them what to do. They were hired," said Mary Sinacore. "As Paterson Habitat grew, it became more and more clear that we needed a paid staff, because it's very hard to rely on volunteers to keep doing the job consistently for a long period of time. So we have an executive director, a bookkeeping person, a volunteer coordinator, and the site coordinators. That really helps keep everything running. And I think that's also a key to our success." Paid positions are both full-time and part-time, depending on what needs to be done and what can be budgeted.

Barbara Dunn, hired as executive director in 1993, had prior nonprofit management experience at Planned Parenthood of Bergen County. "People want nonprofit organizations to run kind of like a corporation, but do so magically with no staff. It's really a balancing act," she said. "If you start to find that you can't find volunteers that have the time or the consistency to get a certain job done, then you start saying, 'OK, maybe I need to pay for part of that.' What you have to be careful of is that you retain the fun part of it, the passion part of it, the spirit of it. I have more volunteers involved now than when I first came. I hope that's a sign that we're doing that OK, that people feel good about the time they give to the organization.

"Because we not only build houses but hold the mortgage on them, we have a whole partnering side of Habitat. We're the construction company and the banker. We've tried to be a nontraditional banker. We're a banker with a heart. We bring in an educational component. We have a lot of different things that happen with that partnering side of it. It means there are many ways for volunteers to become involved," said Dunn, who juggles calls and conferences with bankers and corporate executives on the board of directors, bookkeepers and auditors, carpenters and electricians, college students who stay in a Habitat hostel next to the organization's office in a refurbished factory building, elected officials who can cut through red tape, and news reporters looking for a fresh story. "We're running a business. And you've got to be as effective and as efficient as any other business. Yet, you don't want to become overburdened with

the process. You want people to still really see the excitement and the joy of being involved in a nonprofit. That initial
passion that brought those first few volunteers together—
you want to be able to hold onto that. Because that keeps
you in touch with your mission, keeps you in touch with
the people whose lives you're trying to affect."

Working with a part-time volunteer coordinator and
several office volunteers, Dunn deploys a variety of means
of public outreach. "We use church bulletin announcements
a couple of times a year. It's been a very effective way to get
volunteers," she said. "We do a newsletter about three times
a year. We have almost eleven thousand people on our mailing list. It takes a lot of time to get one newsletter out. As
things grow, it becomes more expensive and more labor-
intensive to get things out. You're torn between trying to
communicate more and spending all your time just communicating. My approach has been that instead of putting
the effort so much into the public relations aspect, I try to
make the program aspect go. If people are excited about the
real things we're doing, it kind of sells itself. Our 'Women's
House' has been a real example of that: a two-year project
funded, designed, and built primarily by women. I got more
publicity out of that without sending out one press release.
It was a different idea for here. It wasn't unique to me. I was
copying something that's been done [elsewhere]. I would
hope that nonprofits would put their time and effort into
making real stuff happen, and then let that real stuff tell its
own story. Once you start heading for that PR angle, you
end up doing things more for image, more for facade. I worry
that the substance starts being diminished. I think it's important that nonprofits tell their own stories in newsletters
and appeal letters, because every time you do that you re-
fine what is it that you're asking of people. If you have
trouble telling your story or putting your message down on

paper, then you have to go back—maybe there's something wrong with your organization. Every time you do an appeal letter or newsletter, it's—what have you done, what's your vision for the future, and how can people get involved? If you just focus on those three items, then people can fit in. They can see whether this is an organization they want to be part of."

To James Staton, a Vietnam War veteran and church deacon disgusted by moral decay in American society as well as the physical decay of his hometown, the Habitat program's religious undertone was appealing. A post office worker living in a cramped apartment with his wife and three children, he applied for a Habitat-built house. After putting in the required five hundred hours of "sweat equity," taking out a mortgage, and moving his family in, he continued as a volunteer. Elected president of the Paterson Habitat Homeowners Association, he set about building community clout with city officials to improve the neighborhood. The Northside's branch library and a bridge to the downtown shopping and civic center had been closed for years. Streets were unswept and seldom patrolled by police. Drug dealers defiantly occupied street corners.

"We went out with picket signs and showed we meant business," said Staton. "Five years ago, there was not adequate policing. We couldn't get deliveries in this area. We couldn't get basic city services—street sweeping and so on. It's been a 180-degree turn. We have community policing. We have deliveries. The library reopened. They redid the bridge and reopened it. All of a sudden, this area has become prime pickings for developers." He credits the beginning of this transformation to the Habitat home builders. "The ice was broken by Habitat," said Staton. But, he added, "it's a community effort. It's not just Habitat homeowners."

To change the attitudes of city officials, Staton found,

first he had to change apathetic attitudes among neighborhood residents. "When I first began, it was only five or six coming to meetings. My vice president, Pedro Ruiz, and I went door to door to homeowners and we asked them to come out to meetings. After we went door to door, it went up to thirty to thirty-five. More and more people got involved." The attendance at community meetings outgrew the initial location in a church basement, then a library room, and eventually required larger space at a neighborhood school.

To keep Habitat homeowners involved and attract other neighborhood residents, Staton utilized his previous experience in American Legion projects that sponsor student essay contests and delegates to Boys State and Girls State. He worked to make community meetings interesting to new homeowners and older neighborhood residents alike. Home Depot experts, for instance, presented workshops on plumbing repairs, window caulking, and other household skills. Raffles and door prizes were offered. Surveys were made of what quality of life issues bothered residents. Plans were developed to find solutions to these issues. "We try to keep it focused on doing positive things in the community," Staton said of the group's monthly meetings. In running meetings, he said, "I make sure there's an agenda. Make sure you cover everything, or you go back to it. I try to keep everything businesslike. If you don't stick to an agenda, you forget about what your focus was." To monitor city council meetings and other citywide events, Staton makes sure someone attends and takes notes. "I can't attend every meeting," he said, reeling off a litany of organizing activities after his workday at the post office. Information of interest to Northside residents is shared at monthly community meetings and via a monthly newsletter. "Communication is one of the key elements" of community organizing, he said.

To Staton, the original goal of Habitat's founders to build houses in an impoverished neighborhood was too limited. The new homeowners, he felt, helped broaden that goal. "The focus was on building houses," he said. "The relationship had to be worked on. The focus has to be on that other part, building the community." Barbara Dunn, who came aboard the Habitat project as executive director several years after it was launched, agrees. "We had a homeowners' association. It was just a place for people to come and talk about problems they were having. To be honest, it really wasn't an effective part of the program," she said. Dunn credits Staton with developing the homeowners' group into an active civic organization.

"This was my first position as executive director. I was trying to learn how to grow in the Habitat organization. And he was simultaneously trying to do this homeowners' organization. We've really helped each other tremendously," she said. "They took surveys of the neighborhood, what people were concerned about. They had about ten things on their first list. They slowly started knocking away. By spearheading things that were already out there, James [Staton] was really able to focus on getting that Arch Street Bridge reopened. They got the North Main library reopened. It was a wonderful vote of confidence by the city. They saw that there were enough citizens that wanted to make change in the neighborhood. I started doing a monthly newsletter for them. The families have taken over the newsletter. It's their newsletter." In a neighborhood that was not served by any newspaper, the homeowners' newsletter provided vital information, said Dunn.

Other key ingredients in the Habitat project are continual public outreach, via speakers and special events, and training of volunteers in a variety of skills. The Paterson Habitat group sends speakers to various religious, social, and business forums armed with large blow-up photos of houses being built by various volunteers, from Girl Scouts to business corporation work teams, statistics on construction costs and fund-raising goals, and lists of past and current contributors likely to be well known to people receiving the presentation. Volunteers who sign up for a day or longer are provided booklets and hands-on instruction on how to install a door frame, for example. The instruction emphasizes safety and working as teams, sharing skills. Each house has an experienced, on-site work supervisor. "The majority of our volunteers are unskilled," says volunteer coordinator Mary Pat Boron, who learned how to organize busy people as a home-school board officer in suburban Ridgewood. "On-the-job training. We want this to be a positive experience and a safe experience. We need to ensure that we have enough supervision. A supervisor is assigned, and they are there to answer any questions and to help them along for the day."

Fund-raisers are also educational events. The group's annual walkathon starts at an overlook of Paterson's awe-inspiring Great Falls and winds through a historic district of former factory buildings that has been revived as housing and shops in recent years, and then crosses the river to the once-forbidding Northside neighborhood and parades past Habitat homes. Along the way, a retired history professor provides commentary on historic sites and events in the "Silk City." At a newly finished Habitat home, a celebratory dedication is held for the family that will move in. "It's just such a nice way to say, 'Welcome to your new home,'" said Mary Pat Boron. It is also an emotionally uplifting, first-hand educational event for volunteers whose sweat and financial contributions made transformation of this neighborhood possible.

"I think one reason that Habitat makes people feel so

good is that you have the concrete—you have the house," said Barbara Dunn. "And it's very easy to measure our success." She is well aware, however, that many civic campaigns tackle problems, such as hunger, that can't be easily measured. From her perspective, every group has to clarify its purpose or it will fail at attracting and keeping volunteers. "Getting together a group of people who feel passionate about something: what is their role?" The best role, she suggests, the model that Habitat for Humanity tries to set, is to help other people to help themselves. "We're still learning how you build community, how you come in as a partner in a community. But, we're at least trying it," she said. "The lessons of the sixties, the War on Poverty, and all those top-down fixes: they don't sustain. You need that local grassroots—the people that are really going to commit to it. But, as Habitat says, you've also got to set up a partnership. Because you need the municipality, you need the business community, you need all the different constituencies. But you've got to have that core of people that live on the street, the neighbors. That's what's going to make a community work. Habitat comes in and works on the local level. But the real grassroots are the families. I see Habitat as trying to plant those seeds."

James Staton, the homeowner leader, feels he learned a lot from Habitat's approach and its eclectic mix of volunteers and staff, suburban and urban residents. "In a project like Habitat, people bring many skills," he said. Many who get attracted to such a project, he added, discover skills they hadn't realized they had or could master with a little guidance. "We're siblings of Habitat. We have become a catalyst ourselves." The homeowners' association is now preparing to build and renovate houses in the Northside neighborhood itself.

Organizing Tips

1. Invite several people to discuss doing a specific community project.
2. Research what has been done elsewhere to gain useful ideas. Share that information in public presentations.
3. Invite people who may have contributed to the problem to participate in the solution and share in the pride of participating in a community creation.
4. Promote the project as a community volunteer effort, with little or no funding expected from government. Invite government officials to participate as volunteers. (They will in turn know where to find government grants, if and when needed.)
5. Encourage family participation. Community projects attract people of all ages.
6. Have fun. Working with neighbors should be enjoyable.
7. Maintain a businesslike schedule. Guide people to balance socializing with working efficiently.
8. Ask people with expertise to train less-experienced volunteers.
9. As the campaign expands, consider whether paid staff makes sense.
10. Periodically review the campaign's goals. Discuss and decide whether course corrections should be made.

3

Saving a

Swamp and

Other

Landmark

Campaigns

Historic save-the-land success stories in America invoke majestic wilderness names: Adirondacks, Yellowstone, Yosemite. Then there's New Jersey. Land of looming garbage mounds, traffic packed highways, flame-belching oil refineries, and the most toxic waste sites in the nation. Yet not far from this dismal landscape are farms and forests, riverbanks and ridges that harbor wildflowers and breathtaking vistas, bald eagles and egrets, black bears and bobcats—astonishing places that were preserved by citizen campaigns and a popular taxpayer-funded Green Acres program.

The fruits of these conservation campaigns include a much-visited wildlife refuge in a swamp once slated to be filled for an airport; canoe and raft trips down a forest-fringed river gorge once slated to be flooded behind an enormous dam; trout fishing in clear-running streams that earlier generations treated as open sewers; and backwoods hiking on trails with rustic views across craggy waves of Appalachian ridges once targeted for sprawling suburban developments.

The Great Swamp Campaign

The granddaddy of these grassroots civic campaigns was the battle to save the Great Swamp. The Port Authority of New York and New Jersey wanted to pave it for a new airport. The neighbors wanted to preserve the marshland, thirty miles west of New York City and less than twenty miles from Newark Airport, for wildlife and their own enjoyment of the rural area's peace and quiet. On one side was the powerful Port Authority, which for decades had bulldozed wherever it wanted to build tunnels, bridges, seaports, and airports to boost the metropolitan region's economy. On the other side were determined citizens who organized a campaign that, over the course of five years, enlisted the support of more than four hundred civic organizations in twenty-nine states, raised more than four million dollars to purchase the core of the land they sought to save, and saw it dedicated as a national wildlife refuge.

All of this was done in the decade before the first Earth Day, in 1970, put environmental issues on the national agenda. "We applaud not action by the federal government," said U.S. Secretary of the Interior Stewart L. Udall at the dedication of the Great Swamp National Wildlife Refuge in May 1964, " . . . but disciplined, tough-minded action by many voluntary citizens groups, who were determined that a unique outdoor place did not have to be sacrificed to the demands of development." To ensure that it would stay undeveloped, Great Swamp supporters mounted a stage-two lobbying action to have the wetlands designated a national wilderness area, which Congress did in 1968. To provide further insurance, supporters convinced Morris and Somerset counties to establish county parks and environmental education centers along refuge borders.

The area, which the Port Authority had insisted was needed to provide a new international airport, was preserved as a rest stop on the East Coast flyway for migratory ducks and geese. Today, the Great Swamp is one of the most visited marshes—by birds and bird-watchers—in the northeast urban corridor. And despite defeat of the airport plan, the Port Authority has continued to service millions of travelers by modernizing its original three major airports in Newark and New York.

The Great Swamp National Wildlife Refuge "is a monument to the many hundreds of persons whose dedication and personal contributions of time, hard work, and financial aid made its accomplishment a reality," noted a historian of the Passaic River, which flows from the swamp into urban New Jersey. Governor Richard J. Hughes, a Democrat who joined with rural Republicans to support the bipartisan effort to save the Great Swamp, hailed the campaign as an "abiding example of citizen action." High praise for a civic campaign run out of local people's homes.

For yet another reason, this was a model grassroots project. Rather than rest on its laurels, the Great Swamp Committee launched a statewide conservation movement, founding the New Jersey Conservation Foundation to help environmental activists around the state save other treasured tracts. The Great Swamp campaign was also carefully documented by participants and recounted in a book. Citizen actions, so often ignored in U.S. history books, seldom are so well recorded.

"Every month some group in the United States faces a sudden proposal—be it a jetport or dam, multipurpose mall or convention center—which would seriously change and disrupt the environment where it is planned," Cam Cavanaugh wrote in *Saving the Great Swamp*, a 1978 account of the citizens' campaign. Offering hard-won lessons for grassroots activists, it presented invaluable insights into how citizens' groups can effectively petition government agencies for assistance. "The Wilderness Society gave the novices from New Jersey helpful suggestions on who to see in Washington, and how to do it: Make a list of people, and call ahead for an appointment. If the legislator is busy, ask who to see. If no one is around, leave a note. Hand out . . . material answering questions which might be raised by that particular person or group. Keep your state's delegation and press informed. Encourage letters to congressmen and senators. Arrange to have speakers at all committee hearings. It was sound common sense advice that took days of effort and plenty of worn shoeleather to accomplish," she noted in a succinct summary of lobbying Congress.

"What lessons are there for citizens groups in general? If the cause is just, if the majority of people are behind the protest, there is much a grassroots movement can, and should, do," she stated, providing a blueprint for effective action: "Publicize the cause. Involve the politicians—and the power brokers. Protest in the media. Get the support of like-minded people and organizations. . . . But equally important, look deeply into your community for the talent, imagination, and good ideas that are surely there. A group of determined people blue-skying ideas and pooling resources can be very effective. If they also pick leaders who are strong and resilient, they will be happily surprised with the results of cooperation."

One of the leaders in the Great Swamp campaign was a

housewife named Helen Fenske, who lived in an old farm-house in Green Village on the edge of the swamp. When the Great Swamp Committee of the North American Wildlife Foundation was formed in 1961, Fenske was named secretary. Since she was a mother of small children, and there wasn't much money to run the organization, the campaign headquarters was set up in a corner of her kitchen over-looking a portion of the wooded wetlands the group wanted to save. "The pastoral view from Helen Fenske's kitchen office was a daily reminder of her cause," noted Cavanaugh. "The kitchen office was soon a beehive of activity, a swinging door of volunteers." Besides coordinating volunteers, Fenske also handled publicity and sallied forth as part of a team of speakers to give talks on the conservation issues to various groups. Seeking wider audiences, she and others organized a display of Great Swamp photos, maps, films, slides, and a re-created pond scene and a marsh botanical garden in the Short Hills Mall. "An estimated 20,000 to 30,000 people saw the exhibit and wanted to learn more about the Great Swamp," wrote Cavanaugh.

"We were constantly looking for creative angles," Fenske later told Cavanaugh. "We needed events that would generate news and project the different aspects of our story. We also wanted it to appear that saving the Great Swamp was a multifaceted issue with vast institutional, governmental, and organizational involvement." Then and since, Great Swamp activists worked hard to win converts to conservation. Many devoted their lives to conservation work.

Having helped coordinate the campaign that ended plans to put airliners practically where her house sat, Fenske continued juggling a busy telephone in her kitchen and dashing out to meetings to help spark other conservation campaigns. She was a founder and executive director of the New Jersey Conservation Foundation. The Ford Foundation hired her to research environmental activism in other states, then underwrote a project she proposed to convince New Jersey lawmakers to follow New England's lead and authorize establishment of municipal conservation committees, creating the framework for what became the Association of New Jersey Environmental Commissions. When the state Department of Environmental Protection (DEP) was created, Fenske was hired in 1970 as special assistant to New Jersey's first environmental commissioner. In 1975, she became special assistant to the head of the U.S. Environmental Protection Agency. Organizing support among environmental groups for Thomas Kean's 1981 campaign for governor, Fenske was appointed an assistant DEP commissioner when Kean won. Near the end of eight years in that post, in January 1990, she served briefly as acting commissioner. Her retirement activities in the nineties included serving as a trustee of the Common Wealth of New Jersey and of the Morris Parks and Land Conservancy, and a director of the Washington Association, a historic preservation organization in Morristown.

"It's a wonderful role, as catalyst. You know, 'been there, done that. Here's what you do. Now do it,'" she chuckled during an interview in the kitchen where history was made. Summing up the Great Swamp campaign more than three decades later, Fenske said: "The key to these [grassroots] organizations is to make everyone feel that they're important to it, giving them a role and giving them credit. Credit is terribly important. We really used to work at that at Great Swamp. Even today, you can sometimes see an obituary and see that the primary thing this man did was save Great Swamp. I think the success of the Great Swamp project is that everyone thought that they had been pivotal in saving Great Swamp. And they were!

"Too often in this field, you have people who want all the credit. One of the things that emerged from Great Swamp was not to let any one person take the credit. Because there are so many," she said. "That project took seven or eight years. Somehow, there was always someone that came forward that opened a door for you, that you couldn't have achieved it if they hadn't been there. How do you say that you're the only one? Little old Fenske out here in this house could never have saved Great Swamp. It became a national issue. The amount of citizen involvement was just incredible—the spirit, the energy, the mix of people at all class levels, working with such commitment and dedication."

Saving the Farny Highlands

Years after the Great Swamp campaign, another conservation effort was launched in a once-remote section of New Jersey now bounded on four sides by busy highways. In the go-go economy of the booming 1980s, housing developments, office complexes, shopping centers, and industrial parks popped up virtually overnight along Garden State roadsides, paving over what for generations had been farm fields and woodlands. Residents of tranquil forest glades began to worry that their way of life was as doomed as that of the wildlife they enjoyed—unless they got busy and organized.

"We were labeled crackpots and cuckoo-birds," Pieter Prall, a Rockaway Township wildlife artist and author, said of the local environmentalists who began challenging big development projects that were on the drawing boards before municipal planning boards in northern Morris County in the mid-1980s. "I grew up here," Prall said, as a reason why he got involved in fighting development plans on behalf of wildlife and rocky water courses. The author of *Birds of North America, Eastern Region* in the Macmillan Field Guide Series, Prall added, "When I was growing up, I spent all my time bird-watching. It was the inspiration for my career. As I was finishing my bird guide [published in 1985], the whole valley along the Beaver Brook—which is recognized as being one of the most valuable habitat sites for some of New Jersey's most threatened and endangered species—was coming under the gun for development."

Many of these projects were initially welcomed by local officials. A decade later, after intense struggles over the fate of rural communities, most of them were dead. Instead of sprawling clusters of condos, golf courses, office buildings, and parking lots, songbirds and soaring hawks, bears, beavers, bobcats, bats, and a great deal of other wildlife still roam the wooded hills rising above the suburban corridors of Interstate Route 80 on the south, Route 287 on the east, and four-lane sections of state highways 15 and 23 on the west and north. How did residents of this rural area, which they named the Farny Highlands, accomplish this—with virtually no news media coverage beyond local newspapers, no celebrities, and little money?

They learned how to reach out to their neighbors, to residents of neighboring towns, to regional conservation groups, to local officials, and to county, state, and federal officials. They expanded the issue from a local, parochial, NIMBY ("not in my backyard") concern to a regional one of clean water supplies and habitat for endangered wildlife. And they sought out experienced conservation activists like Helen Fenske willing to share their expertise.

"It's been a huge success," said Fenske, who championed the Farny Highlands campaign as assistant commissioner at the Department of Environmental Protection and in her retirement role as an advisor to various civic campaigns. "It's been a rather remarkable coalition. There are a number of people who worked for this for a number of years." None of them were household names. The strength of the Farny Highlands Coalition was provided by people who live in the area and supporters in unheralded posts with county, state, and federal agencies. Fenske credited employees of the DEP's Parks and Forestry, Green Acres, and Fish, Game, and Wildlife offices, Morris County Park Commission, Jersey City and Newark watershed agencies, National Park Service, and U.S. Fish and Wildlife Service. But the organizers who pressed the issue were local residents.

At first, they felt overwhelmed by the idea of tackling powerful real estate interests that suddenly targeted their sparsely settled communities. Brushing aside conservation concerns, developers saw a landscape ripe for suburban development. Despite a court-ordered temporary building ban in the 1970s after the Rockaway River upstream of the Jersey City reservoir in Parsippany was polluted by sewage from overdevelopment along the Route 80 corridor, proposed large-scale housing and office building projects were lined up for forest tracts in the adjacent hills in the 1980s like jetliners ready for takeoff at the expanding Newark Airport.

Looking for allies, members of local environmental groups began comparing notes. They soon realized that they didn't have the resources, time, or political clout to fight each project on their own—let alone fight several development projects simultaneously. "We were all going to planning board meetings and disputing developers' plans," said Prall. "We all of a sudden realized that what we had to do was get the land bought. We could have fought forever and not saved any land." The solution that was arrived at was to form a regional coalition, seek the support of state and federal environmental agencies, and give a name to the forested area that sprawls across the top of Morris County and spills over into part of Sussex County. More than thirty organizations—garden clubs, hiking clubs, conservation groups—joined the coalition once it was organized in 1991.

"The Farny Highlands, like Sterling Forest, was threatened. It was in equal jeopardy," recalled Lorraine Caruso, a biology professor at William Paterson University and former member of the Denville Environmental Commission, past president of the Morris Highlands Audubon Society, and League to Save Open Space director, who, like many Farny Highlands activists, wore many hats in a determined effort to build an effective conservation network. Sterling Forest, on the New York–New Jersey border, was a save-the-land poster child championed by two governors and numerous members of Congress, whose preservation campaign was trumpeted in the New York metropolitan news media. The Farny Highlands, in contrast, was a poor country cousin, whose fate was chronicled only in local newspapers. Its salvation was up to embattled residents trying to figure out what to do to preserve their neck of the woods. The first thing they realized they needed to do was to give their beloved ridges a name, so they could tell the outside world what they wanted to save.

Joan Lisi of Denville's Protect Our Wetlands, Water, and Woods suggested the name Farny Highlands, after Major George Farny, the state's first planner, who once owned land in the area. Diane Nelson, a Boonton Township resident who worked for the Morris County Park Commission, compiled a carefully researched booklet and maps that detailed the natural features of undeveloped tracts across the region and their relationship to watershed streams feeding reservoirs.

The documents and maps delineated the craggy ridges and trout streams that form the wooded watershed for Jersey City's reservoirs located in Parsippany and Rockaway Township. They showed wetlands and the underlying aquifer that supplies town wells across the region. They showed that the area's northern border abuts the city of Newark's reservoir lands, which in turn abut the Wanaque Reservoir watershed, which stretches into Sterling Forest in New York.

They presented the Farny Highlands as the source of drinking water for a third of North Jersey residents and part of a greenway of forests across the top of the Garden State that helps provide clean air on the edge of the East Coast metropolis while hosting hundreds of species of plants and animals, including many listed as threatened or endangered.

Nelson's work impressed state environmental officials, who used it to line up funding support. "Diane put together a sort of master plan for the Farny Highlands," said David Epstein, executive director of the Morris Parks and Land Conservancy, a nonprofit agency that helped to coordinate this campaign, from which it grew into a countywide force in conservation work. "Diane Nelson pulled together the most wonderful loose-leaf booklet and maps. No one had ever pulled it all together," said Helen Fenske. "She gave it to everyone in DEP who might have anything to do with Farny. What the state saw was that this was 30 percent of the state's water supply" in North Jersey. "The state saw its interest was to protect the water supply."

Fenske was acutely aware that the Great Swamp campaign had been launched without any environmental data base or thought about protecting the marsh from the effects of development outside its borders. Only later did Great Swamp advocates realize the research they needed to do to convince neighboring communities to save the new wildlife refuge from being polluted and filled in by silty runoff from upstream development. So she was glad to see that the case for preserving headwaters, forested slopes, and stream corridors in the Farny Highlands was well documented.

Early on, at the request of local environmental groups, a study by the U.S. Fish and Wildlife Service recommended that a national wildlife preserve be created centered on the Beaver Brook area in Rockaway Township. Federal funds were not available for such a project, however. The search for funding turned to Trenton. At DEP headquarters, the state Green Acres program was inundated with a dozen or more separate requests for aid to preserve various sites in the Farny region. "They all came in with their own projects, their own maps," Fenske recalled. To sort out what could be realistically done, a strategy meeting was held. During that meeting, representatives of various groups colored in on one large map areas that they would take responsibility for preserving. And then, with a common sense of purpose and a common strategy, the members of the Farny Highlands Coalition went home and renewed their efforts.

A key part of those efforts was showing the public what was at stake. To entice visitors to view tracts the campaign wanted to preserve, volunteers created the Farny Highlands Trail Network. One trail starts in the former iron-mining hamlet of Hibernia, barely a couple of miles from Route 80 traffic, yet in another world. The path lures hikers up mossy outcroppings into a craggy forest that was slated for development into five golf course communities. It is now the core of a two-thousand-acre conservation area called Wildcat Ridge. The trail winds up and down forested ridges, passing stone remains of abandoned iron-mining works, caves inhabited by rare Indiana bats, lichen-covered rock formations created by the last Ice Age.

"Waters passing through the rugged cliffs and forests in this glacially scoured region ultimately flow to the Passaic, Delaware, and Hudson rivers," notes a hikers' guide created by the Morris Parks and Land Conservancy and the New York–New Jersey Trail Conference. "One trail volunteer noted a recurring pattern in his wildlife observations. . . . In the oak-hardwood forests, he saw North American wild turkeys. On the exposed cliff regions, he observed red-tailed hawks. The great blue heron inhabited the wetlands." Helping to blaze a trail through the region, another volunteer excitedly remarked that this is "a part of New Jersey rarely experienced by anyone. You'd think you were in northern Canada!"

Many coalition members focused their efforts on local projects they felt were especially crucial, while networking with activists in neighboring towns. Seeking to save Pyramid Mountain in the northeast section of the region from bulldozers, Lucy Meyer in Kinnelon, for example, built local support step-by-step to press for Green Acres purchase of the mountain. When that was accomplished, she turned her attention, and that of her town, to adjacent tracts. By all accounts, Meyer's low-key determination inspired many other conservation activists. Helen Fenske admired Meyer for "her persistence. She just wouldn't give up. She's one of my heroines."

To raise money to qualify for state Green Acres and Morris County open space fund matching grants, Prall the artist and Caruso the biologist teamed up with Boonton Township businessman and conservationist Kip Koehler (who died of cancer in 1996) to sow the seeds for establishing municipal land trusts. By 1997, nearly every town in the region had a land trust funded by a small dedicated municipal tax on property owners. That year, the Green Acres program culminated a round of negotiations on the most recent of a series of purchases of more than 4,800 acres in the Farny Highlands for $11.5 million. Many of these purchases were done jointly with conservation groups and local towns.

As battles erupted in Congress over providing taxpayer funds to help buy 15,000 acres in Sterling Forest, the coalition of conservation groups and Green Acres officials quietly negotiated the purchase of, or conservation easements on, nearly half of the 35,000-acre Farny Highlands. That work continued through the 1990s, with the goal of buying small properties that link a patchwork of large preserved tracts, in order to conserve contiguous stretches of forested ridges and stream corridors.

In an age of mega-coverage of selected save-the-earth campaigns, here is another kind of civic success story. Instead of pilgrimages by national political figures to get televised amid Sterling Forest's rugged beauty, the Farny Highlands campaign drew the fierce support of local folks. Across the seven-town region, more than 16,000 acres have been preserved as state lands, county and town parks, as well as Scout camps and reservoir lands that have conservation easements. Negotiations continued in 1998 for another 1,200 acres. The remaining 18,000 acres of forest are listed on a master plan for conservation efforts.

A number of conservation groups became working partners in acquiring lands in the region. These included local groups—Beaverbrook Watershed Conservancy, Boonton Township Environmental Committee, Citizen Action Committee of Mt. Hope, Friends of Pyramid Mountain, League to Save Open Space, Protect Our Wetlands, Water and Woods, Rockaway Township Environmental Commission, Tourne Valley Coalition, and the Upper Rockaway River Watershed Association; regional organizations—Garden Club of America Zone IV, Morris County Park Commission, Morris Parks and Land Conservancy, and the Passaic River Coalition; state organizations—Association of New Jersey Environmental Commissions, Common Wealth of New Jersey, New Jersey Audubon Society, and New Jersey Conservation Foundation; and interstate and national organizations—New York–New Jersey Trail Conference, Nature Conservancy, and Trust for Public Land.

"It has been grassroots lobbying at its best," said David Epstein. "You had all these disparate groups with totally different objectives. A lot of them didn't know each other; some of them didn't like each other. But by coming together, they brought a lot of power to the table. That's how this effort was successful."

"It was an incredible amount of work," said Pieter Prall, who focused his efforts in Rockaway Township. "There are probably one hundred thousand hours of work over ten years." Among other things, he said, dozens of volunteers "knocked on every door in this town several times with petitions," in order to change the climate at town hall to support Green Acres, create a municipal land trust, and help purchase threatened sites. Nor is the hard work over. "A lot of the lands that are protected are patchwork. There's lots of holes," said Epstein. "The state just focuses on the big pieces. They're not going after those little pieces. It's going to be a challenge for the Farny Highlands Coalition to fill in all the gaps in those missing pieces."

"We haven't accomplished the goal—the goal being to purchase as much as possible—but we're getting there," said Lorraine Caruso. Looking ahead, Caruso has shifted her focus to public education about the needs of wildlife in the preserved forests. What is needed, she insists, is a deeper sense of "environmental ethics," of respect by hikers and trail bikers for nesting places and other critical habitats, once woodlands have been saved from development. "I would say we were pretty successful, thanks to the staff at Green Acres," said Diane Nelson, who created the report on the Farny Highlands that impressed state officials. "We gave them a strategy. That was part of the secret of success." Nelson, a trustee of the Upper Rockaway River Watershed Association, said the coalition was "an excellent group. Many of the people are still involved, looking at larger Highlands issues."

Summing up what he learned about environmental activism from the Farny Highlands campaign, Pieter Prall said, "What I'm finding out is there are stages to a project. There is the activist stage; then the bureaucratic stage, where the agencies get involved and buy land; and there is the political stage, where the politicians come in at the end and tell everyone how they saved everything." From the perspective of having worked in grassroots campaigns and in government, Helen Fenske said, "You need both. You need government and you need the catalyst. You need the public. The public's always ahead of government. They see the need, they see the issues, first. You need citizen organizations to complain and get the issues out there. But they do not, for the most part, make the basic decisions, or get the money that makes things finally happen. There is a process of decision making. A great many environmental groups, especially new ones, don't understand that process." Part of that process, she said, is learning how to gain the ear and then the support of bureaucrats and politicians "in a timely fashion, before decisions are made."

Fenske's advice to citizen groups is to learn how local, county, state, and federal government function, in order to make use of government resources and decision-making powers. Too often, she said, local residents and community groups concerned about environmental issues don't get involved in the political process until after a decision they don't like has been made. Conservationists, she said, "should be involved" in the political arena. "Too many say, 'I don't like politics.' You need people with good relations with government."

Having survived the pressure cooker of state politics, where environmental matters are usually in danger of being pushed aside in the jockeying of competing interest groups during election campaigns and day-to-day governing, Fenske advises conservation groups to be persistent in making their case to government agencies, elected officials, political candidates, the public, and the news media. "The press is key," she said, to concentrating public attention on an issue. And the key to the press, she tells grassroots groups, is crafting an effective press release and making calls that convey the specifics of a particular environmental concern to busy journalists. Yet headlines and television coverage, she cautions, only put civic activists in the arena; they don't guarantee success.

Land conservation in the nation's most urbanized state, she emphasizes, is the result of unrelenting hard work. "One of the things I think I learned over the years," said Fenske, "is that you work for incremental progress, and not for total victory all in a flash. Some activists feel you have to go for 100 percent. You can't always get 100 percent. You have to settle, sometimes, for say 25 percent. And then you go for another bite. You have to stick with it."

As Farny Highlands Coalition members learned, the responsiveness of the public and government officials to a citizen-led conservation effort owed a big debt to the legacy of the Great Swamp campaign. Thirty years after the Great Swamp campaign, Governor Christine Todd Whitman led a press tour of the Great Swamp National Wildlife Refuge to plug its role as a key element in her administration's tourism advertising campaign. Remarking that she could spend "a lifetime" amid so much natural beauty, Whitman lauded the "grassroots effort it took to preserve this place."

On another day, at a press conference at another wilderness tract saved by a citizen campaign, the governor again praised the work of grassroots environmental activists. "I cannot overstate the significance of this occasion and enterprise," Whitman said at a June 1994 ceremony at Pyramid Mountain, a wooded peak rising above a reservoir on the eastern edge of the Farny Highlands thirty-three miles due west of Manhattan, where she signed legislation appropriating nearly $34 million for preservation of more than 20,000 acres of forests and other unpaved tracts in various parts of the state. "We cannot take the clean air and water supply that we need for granted," she said. "So it is an ecological imperative that we put a premium on preservation."

Whitman, a business-booster Republican elected in a taxpayer revolt against her Democratic predecessor, repeatedly paid tribute to the state's Green Acres program, which since 1961 had provided over $1 billion in taxpayer-backed bonds to purchase more than 310,000 acres for parks and nature preserves. Convinced by conservationists that not nearly enough was being done to preserve areas such as the Farny Highlands from the increased pace of development, Whitman in 1998 proposed a $1 billion bonding plan to preserve one million acres of farmlands and forests, wetlands and river corridors, or about half of all the open space left in the state. Voters approved this costly plan by a 2–1 margin, a move that drew national news media attention to New Jersey's shift to set limits on suburban sprawl.

It's a good indicator that a grassroots campaign has taken root when a state's top elected official backs the cause. In a small state like New Jersey, civic campaigns on statewide or regional issues that build a groundswell of public support are likely to get a governor's attention. For politicians the attraction of championing a popular project is obvious—the hope that voters will associate them with a worthy cause. The payoff for a citizens' campaign is that governors are good at focusing issues for legislators and the news media. And, in making regional or national appeals, they carry clout with leaders of neighboring states and with members of Congress.

Campaign to Save Sterling Forest

The campaign to save Sterling Forest from development was launched by several grassroots conservation groups in New York and New Jersey in the late 1980s during a boom time in speculative development of office complexes and housing tracts in remote areas near interstate highways. Sterling Forest stretches along both sides of the New York–New Jersey border a few miles west of a new intersection of Route 287 and the New York State Thruway that was scheduled to open in the early 1990s. Sterling Forest featured ski slopes, a cluster of bucolic corporate campuses and conference centers, and miles of wooded peaks that have been likened to a northern rain forest, harboring bears, eagles, and numerous species of neotropical songbirds that winter in Central America. Swiss and Swedish investment companies bought the forest and were intent on building a small city amid this lush landscape. Besides being a major wildlife habitat on the edge of the New York megalopolis, the mountain forest provides rain and snow runoff to New Jersey's major reservoir system, which supplies water for two million residents and thousands of businesses across North Jersey.

Given this combination of elements, the "Save Sterling Forest" campaign easily generated a lot of news media attention and public support. But its organizers found they would need to raise a lot of money to buy the land, in a period during which the federal government had cut back on funding conservation causes. The grassroots campaign got a boost when it was endorsed by the North Jersey District Water Supply Commission, which operates the Wanaque Reservoir system on behalf of cities and towns in several counties, and elected officials in many North Jersey communities and their representatives in Congress. It got another boost when the Passaic County freeholders condemned the New Jersey portion, which borders a reservoir, and bought some 2,000 acres for $9 million, aided with state Green Acres funds.

It got another crucial boost when Governor Whitman signed a bipartisan bill passed by the New Jersey Legislature authorizing $10 million to help purchase more than 15,000 acres of forest in New York for $55 million. Explaining why New Jersey should send money to a neighboring state, Whitman cited the precedent of New York helping New Jersey save the Hudson River Palisades from quarry operations at the beginning of the twentieth century and in jointly creating the Palisades Interstate Park Commission (PIPC), which manages a popular bistate park that extends along the Hudson River and curves inland across New York's Hudson Highlands to one edge of Sterling Forest. There was no outcry by taxpayer watchdog groups over this action in Trenton to help preserve a cross-border source of clean water supplies.

Many New Jersey residents were well aware of a previous popular bistate conservation campaign. Not long after the Great Swamp Committee's success in the 1960s, another grassroots campaign halted a plan to dam the upper Delaware River near the Delaware Water Gap to create a water supply reservoir. Tackling the Army Corps of Engineers, which built dams all across America, a determined group of citizens outmaneuvered a very powerful federal agency. They created a model of civic cooperation across state lines, bridging remote regions of New Jersey and Pennsylvania. They enlisted the support of the National Park Service for a free-flowing river as the centerpiece of a new national park that would feature canoeing, white-water rafting, and riverside camping within day-trip distance from the New York and Philadelphia metropolitan regions. They contacted the news media to spotlight Army Corps of Engineers actions in evicting riverbank residents and bulldozing historic colonial-era stone homes. And, turning anger into action, they mobilized thousands upon thousands of supporters to write, call, telegram, and visit Congress.

Responding to unrelenting protests by New Jersey and Pennsylvania residents, and by visitors from other states who signed petitions circulated at the National Park Service visitors center just off Route 80 in the Delaware Water Gap, Congress in 1978 placed the endangered section of river in the National Wild and Scenic Rivers System. The winning combination was created by local residents and national conservation groups who formed the Save the Delaware Coalition. Orchestrating persistent protests, astute solicitation of news media coverage, well-informed testimony at hearings, and old-fashioned lobbying, "this umbrella organization became strong enough to command the respect of Congress," Frank Dale, a regional historian, noted in *Delaware Diary*. "A turning point came when the governors of the four states in the valley and a representative of the Department of the Interior met in Newark, New Jersey, in July 1975. They voted 3–1 against further funding for the Tocks Dam. . . . Only Pennsylvania held out for what was fast becoming a lost cause," Dale recounted.

Even with this precedent, the Sterling Forest campaign faced a hard struggle. "There were a lot of stumbling blocks" in getting New York and New Jersey officials to cooperate with each other, recalled Ella Filippone, head of the Passaic River Coalition, one of several New Jersey conservation groups that worked with counterparts in New York for a decade to line up such a constellation of government support. "If New Jersey hadn't put up that $10 million, I don't think Sterling Forest would have been saved," said Filippone, who gained Whitman's respect and public praise for unrelenting work lining up legislative support. A key part of the funding strategy was that New Jersey's $10 million pledge presented a challenge to New York to match it, while both states pressed the federal government to also chip in. A big stumbling block was that Trenton and New York City were waging fierce turf battles over who got prestigious corporate offices, professional sports teams, and bragging rights to Ellis Island. Campaign activists had to diplomatically build a network of supportive Republican and Democratic elected officials in two hotly competitive states.

At the same time, they had to cobble together a coalition of contentious conservationists. The Sterling Forest campaign was launched by several grassroots environmental groups that had a common goal of preserving a mountain forest. That's what brought the Appalachian Mountain Club, the New York–New Jersey Trail Conference, and several New Jersey conservation groups to create the Sterling Forest Coalition in 1988. But groups joined for various reasons. Some joined because of the forest's role as a source of clean water for New Jersey. Some were drawn by its role as shelter for migratory songbirds and other wildlife. And some championed its outdoors recreational role as host of a section of the Georgia-to-Maine Appalachian Trail.

In addition, there were differences over the campaign's focus and over basic strategy and tactics. "There was a split in the environmental community on Sterling, between New York groups and New Jersey groups," said Jeff Tittel, executive director of the New Jersey Sierra Club, who was a founder of the Sterling Forest campaign. New York groups, he said, mainly focused on saving Sterling Forest, while New Jersey groups viewed the forest as one piece in a greenway they want to create across the region. The greenway issue was pressed in New Jersey by an umbrella group called the Highlands Coalition, which supports conservation of what hasn't already been developed in a seven-county region stretching from the Delaware River to the New York border at Sterling Forest. "Some in the New Jersey side were concerned that if all the legislation and monies were focused on Sterling, then we would lose the bigger picture. The [New York] people felt that if we went after a big chunk of the Highlands, it would jeopardize getting money for Sterling," said Tittel.

Despite these fundamental differences, the campaign continued to draw more and more supporters, including many municipal and county officials concerned about water supplies and ordinary citizens concerned about traffic jams and other effects of unfettered sprawl. The nonprofit Regional Plan Association issued a report advocating the preservation of a greenbelt across the entire New York–New Jersey Highlands with Sterling Forest as its buckle. The Palisades Interstate Park Commission offered to manage the forest once it was purchased and added its lobbying weight in state and federal government circles. Letters and phone calls from thousands of people in both states enlisted the support of Whitman and her Republican counterpart, New York Governor George Pataki, and members of Congress from both states.

The strength of the Sterling Forest Coalition was its wide base of persistent grassroots activism by groups and individuals who felt the forest should be preserved for a variety of reasons. Coordination of a fractious coalition spread across two states was provided by a hired campaign director, John Gebhards, who produced numerous forums, hiking events, and a stream of newsletters to promote the issue and provide updates on the course of the campaign. Additional coordination of the campaign, focused on networking with government officials and other major fundraising sources, was provided by the Palisades Interstate Park

Commission's executive director, Robert Binnewies. Leaders of grassroots groups credited Binnewies with transforming fractious coalition meetings into a well-focused campaign. He set the pace and professional tone for raising the issue repeatedly with officials in Albany, Trenton, and Washington.

"Bob Binnewies made innumerable visits to Congress" to lobby committee chairmen and other key members of the House and Senate, said a Palisades Interstate Park commissioner from New Jersey. "As I did," added the commissioner, one of many Sterling Forest supporters who worked quietly behind the scenes, while others promoted their involvement with press conferences. "I don't get paid to be a commissioner," he said. "I was doing this on my time." Besides volunteering their time to lobby for this conservation effort, PIPC commissioners and their friends raised funds to hire experts to counter the Sterling Forest development plan and spark buyout negotiations. "There were many people of substantial means who never wanted their names to be known who contributed substantial amounts of money," said the commissioner. "The lesson to be learned," he said, "is that it took an enormous effort by an enormous number of people from all walks of life."

The search to secure state and federal funds, which helped attract foundation and private contributions, was conducted by a widespread coalition. What grassroots groups like the Appalachian Mountain Club, New Jersey Conservation Foundation, New Jersey Audubon Society, New York–New Jersey Trail Conference, Passaic River Coalition, Sierra Club, Skylands CLEAN, and many others brought to bear was the energy and passion and potential votes of thousands of volunteers. These groups invested years of effort in the Sterling Forest campaign, in addition to their own projects. The Passaic River Coalition, for instance, was formed to prod government agencies to upgrade sewage treatment plants and halt harmful runoff that polluted the Passaic River and its tributaries supplying regional water supplies. In alliance with the North Jersey District Water Supply Commission, the river-watch group argued that development in the headwaters in Sterling Forest threatened clean water gains downstream.

Garden State conservation groups also brought a legacy of accomplishments—cleaner streams and rivers, for instance, where they had focused public attention that prodded government and industry action. They brought years of experience in dealing with government agencies, both in terms of gaining allies and countering with creative ideas and vocal grassroots coalitions such plans as damming the scenic upper Delaware River promoted by some agencies. Over a three-decade period, from the 1970s into the 1990s, conservation groups spearheaded grassroots opposition to Army Corps of Engineers' plans to provide flood control along the meandering Passaic River and its tributaries with sprawling networks of first dams, then massive Mississippi-style levees, and finally a $2 billion complex of flood tunnels designed to flush rising rivers from suburban backyards up in the hills underground twenty miles out to Newark Bay. Each successive flood-control plan was countered by conservationists' arguments that it would be less expensive and more effective to buy out riverbank homes that had been built in the river system's floodplain, and that, furthermore, flooding into wetlands throughout the region recharges underground water supplies for wells used in many communities.

During a prolonged rainy season in the Midwest in 1993, widespread destructive flooding was caused by runoff trapped behind the levees built by the Corps of Engineers, dramatically demonstrating that engineers don't always have the solution to coping with natural events. Presented with a well-researched alternative to the Corps of Engineers' plans, New Jersey officials under the Whitman administration shifted their flood-control focus for the Passaic River basin from dams, levees, and tunnels to the buyout and riverbank and wetlands conservation plan proposed by the Passaic River Coalition and other conservation groups.

The Sterling Forest campaign had to confront another barrier—this one political—often encountered in dealing with governments. Just as campaign organizers and supporters had lined up support of Democratic governors in Albany and Trenton, Republicans won election to those posts. Just as campaign workers had warmed up support in the Democratic Clinton administration in Washington, Republicans won control of Congress. At both the state and federal levels, just as some funding seemed secured, a new cast of key officials had to be lobbied. Frustrations mounted. Funding bills in Congress sponsored by New Jersey and New York Democrats died for lack of Republican support. Funding bills sponsored by New York and New Jersey Republicans died for lack of support by Republicans from other states.

Sterling Forest abruptly became a national symbol of conservation when a renewed bipartisan request to Congress in 1996 to help buy the forest sparked bitter wrangling between western and eastern representatives over the federal government's ownership of vast tracts in western states. The congressional debate over whether there are too many national parks propelled a parade of federal officials to visit Sterling Forest, with television cameras in tow, to burnish their environmental credentials in the eyes of voters. Democratic and Republican representatives from New York, New Jersey, and the Speaker of the House, who hailed from Georgia, jockeyed with Clinton administration officials to appear in newspaper photos and on television standing with conservationists next to one of the New Jersey reservoirs with Sterling Forest rising in the background. "Interior Secretary Bruce Babbitt came to Sterling on Earth Day 1996 to announce that President Clinton was making the forest a centerpiece of his 'Parks for Tomorrow' plan. House Speaker Newt Gingrich [Clinton's dogged political foe] also visited the forest, promising to unfetter federal funding," noted a report by the Trust for Public Land, a key negotiator in the buyout campaign.

But to pry money out of a fiscally conservative, Republican-dominated Congress, the Sterling Forest campaign had to show it could raise a good portion of its buyout package from the two affected states. Despite years of lobbying, however, neither New York nor New Jersey had allocated funds for purchasing the forest. A strategy was devised to get Trenton to challenge Albany to put up some serious money and jointly press Washington to match it. The idea came from coalition activists experienced in the ways of leveraging various levels of government to create the means to accomplish a grassroots goal.

"They all laughed at me when I first said we may have to spend money in another state to protect our water supply. But it did come to fruition. We worked it through the [New Jersey] legislature," said Ella Filippone. First, campaign supporters sought and gained a legislative resolution of support for saving Sterling Forest. This didn't cost the lawmakers anything and was for a popular cause. "It flew through," said Filippone. With the legislature on record as backing the preservation of Sterling Forest, campaign activists and savvy supporters in state government sought to leverage that support to get some money. Astute research had previously ferreted out some unspent bond monies held in trust for conservation of watersheds. Now, conservationists and legislative allies asked that $10 million from the bond monies be dedicated to the Sterling Forest buyout fund. With Governor Whitman eager to sign such a historic appropriation, it was granted by a Republican-dominated legislature not always noted for taking a conservation stance.

With that, fund-raising took off. New York put up $16 million. After furious debate and cliffhanger votes, Congress provided $17.5 million. The Lila Acheson and DeWitt Wallace Fund for the Hudson Highlands donated $5 million. The Doris Duke Charitable Foundation also donated $5 million. The Victoria Foundation, which usually gave grants only to projects in New Jersey, provided $1 million. Students at Dwight D. Eisenhower Middle School in Wyckoff, New Jersey, raised $158. A Sterling Forest fund campaign at the E. G. Hewitt Elementary School in Ringwood raised $1,034.74. A group of college students raised $5,000 with a bike-a-thon. Other school groups, foundations, and private citizens contributed thousands more dollars.

Campaign insiders credited New Jersey with leading the way: first, by helping Passaic County purchase the Garden State section of the forest, then pledging $10 million and challenging New York to match it, and forming a bistate request for federal funds to help buy the bulk of the forest in New York. After more than a year of parallel purchase negotiations and fund-raising, the wooded ridges that had been slated for a small city of housing developments and office complexes became a New York State park in 1998.

"We're not finished yet," said Ella Filippone, referring to a remaining 2,200-acre portion the owners kept with plans for a scaled-down development, which environmentalists want to see preserved as parkland. "But we're at a landmark spot." Other campaign activists, such as Jeff Tittel, felt it would be premature to declare victory until the final portion of the forest is preserved. Some felt the piecemeal approach to purchasing segments of the forest was not the best strategy.

"The goal we set for ourselves in the beginning was to acquire all of Sterling Forest," said Tittel, who got involved in the conservation campaign as a leader of Skylands CLEAN, a grassroots environmental group in Ringwood, a northern New Jersey community that hosts the Wanaque and Monksville reservoirs that lie just downslope from Sterling Forest. Tittel had argued that government agencies on the New York side should have acted, as Passaic County did on the New Jersey side, to acquire the forest under the legal power of eminent domain and then work out in court how much to pay for the land at fair market prices. New York state officials ruled out that approach and instead engaged two nonprofit land conservancy organizations, the Trust for Public Land and the Open Space Institute, to negotiate a buyout with representatives of the European landowners.

"[Governor] Pataki brought in outside negotiators, who were under pressure to make a quick deal. All in all, it made the rush to get this thing done for political and financial reasons [hurried] to the point where the other side had a total upper hand," said Tittel. "Then a deal was signed, and we couldn't see it. We had to get a Freedom of Information Act request to see it. We found out they kept the logging rights for six months beyond [the sale], where they got quite a bit of money destroying forest. We found they kept the water rights. And, more importantly, they kept the choicest, most developable property, right along the road. It makes access to the interior of the forest almost nonexistent. They get to keep 2,200 acres in the center where all the road access is."

Tittel, Filippone, and other grassroots activists who worked hard for a decade to save Sterling Forest were nearly lost amid the standing-room-only crowd at a celebratory press conference at which Governors Pataki and Whitman and other officials took center stage when the $55 million buyout deal was announced. "So all the politicians got up and patted themselves on the back saying, 'We saved Sterling Forest.' When in fact, it's like a giant C with the core of the C being owned by Sterling Forest Corporation," said Tittel. "All in all, we had to support it because it was the only deal we got. But it really was a bad deal. And now we've got environmental groups saying, 'Well, we got most of it; instead of wasting money up there, let's use the money for something else.' Again, it's because of different factions, different groups losing sight of what the goal was."

Yet, for all the anguished, publicly expressed concerns of grassroots conservationists like Tittel—and perhaps because of such persistent criticism—momentum toward a clearly defined goal had been created that would be hard to stop. Amid ongoing debate and sometimes bitter disagreement over strategy and tactics, leaders of the Sterling Forest Coalition vowed to continue their campaign until the remaining portion is purchased. Governor Pataki pledged to accomplish that goal.

Whatever the final resolution of the parcel still in dispute, the Sterling Forest Coalition over the course of a decade accomplished a lot. Step by step, it engineered the purchase of 90 percent of Sterling Forest. It got the governor of New York on record pledging to preserve the rest. The issue of preserving lands such as Sterling Forest from suburban sprawl grew from a local grassroots campaign into a national issue embraced by the Clinton administration, the anti-Clinton Speaker of the House, and many other elected officials in both major parties. The idea of a greenbelt extending across the New Jersey–New York Highlands, with Sterling Forest as the buckle, grew from a grassroots idea into the focus of a Regional Plan Association report that was heralded in the *New York Times* and other metropolitan newspapers. To provide institutional muscle for the idea, the New Jersey legislature authorized the Palisades Interstate Park Commission, which manages Bear Mountain, Sterling Forest, and other wilderness parklands in New York's Hudson Highlands, to expand its jurisdiction into the New Jersey Highlands.

At the New York–New Jersey Trail Conference office in Manhattan, Executive Director JoAnn Dolan, another of the founders of the Sterling Forest campaign, felt the bistate coalition had produced invaluable lessons to share with others doing conservation work. "We have learned that environmental groups with very different agendas can work together strategically and come up with very potent results if we pool our resources and keep our eye on the mission," Dolan stated in a summary of the Sterling Forest campaign published in the hiking group's newsletter. "Now, we have created a model for future projects—like protecting the Highlands of New Jersey and New York."

Another perspective was provided by politicians who embraced the conservationists' cause. "This is a model of how the government and private sector can work together to preserve our nation's environmental quality," Representative Marge Roukema, a Republican Congresswoman from North Jersey who repeatedly sponsored funding bills, stated in a press release marking a milestone in federal and state fund-raising for buying the forest. "I worked for many years to secure federal funding for Sterling Forest, only to encounter obstacle after obstacle," she said. "We finally did it. It just goes to show how perseverance and determination works. . . . This project has succeeded because government officials have set aside political and regional differences to work together and, in turn, to work with the private sector."

Robert Torricelli, another longtime supporter of the Sterling Forest campaign as a Democratic member of Congress from Bergen County and then a United States senator, called a strategy meeting of conservationists in the wake of the Sterling Forest buyout press conferences. On a sunny midday atop a scenic bank of the Wanaque Reservoir, Senator Torricelli sat amid a small cluster of picnic tables with grassroots activists from New Jersey and New York conservation groups and discussed the nuts and bolts of conducting a wider campaign to preserve the bistate Highlands region. In various other meetings of civic activists across the region, the next stage was being launched.

Organizing Tips

1. Citizen campaigns can be run at minimal cost from participants' homes. Networking with nonprofit groups, religious institutions, and local officials can provide meeting rooms for large public gatherings when needed.
2. Brainstorming sessions help set campaign goals, create a campaign name, craft a workable strategy, outline necessary actions, and decide who does what.
3. Civic campaigns run on ideas that, if they creatively address the issue, attract financial and other sorts of support.
4. Set and follow a step-by-step, persistent approach to gaining public support and, ultimately, government action. People are attracted to civic campaigns that demonstrate momentum, offer creative events, and have confident, knowledgeable leadership. Form a coalition that has multiple leaders representing member groups.
5. Parcel out responsibilities, depending on skills and interest of volunteers, for research, public outreach, press

contacts, letter writing, phone trees, petitions, fund-raising, lobbying, and campaign coordination.

6. Train coalition members to present cogent, fact-based arguments at public forums, press interviews, and meetings with government officials.

7. Provide clearly written, concisely organized, well-researched materials, maps, and photos to government officials, news media, and the public. Present this information in creative ways that catch people's attention and cause them to think about the issues being raised.

8. Make your case respectfully and consistently to all possible supporters and opponents. Civic campaigns are won by gaining converts, not battlefield body counts.

9. Don't rely on government officials to set the parameters of a civic campaign. Utilize whatever assistance officials can provide, thank them for their contributions, and persistently continue advancing the next step and the next step and the next step toward the long-range goal.

10. Share the accolades for each accomplishment and give credit where credit is due.

4

Better Living

through

Mutual-Help

Groups

Citizen campaigns come in all sorts of shapes and sizes. Many well-known ones address external threats to the health of a community and its environment. Some less well known ones address internal problems. Many Americans beset by physical handicaps, post-traumatic stress, survivor grief, psychological ailments, learning disabilities, and age-related conditions that doctors, hospitals, and other institutions can't entirely cure have discovered the healing power of community-based mutual-aid self-help groups composed of people with similar problems. This is an arena that has steadily grown in recent years outside the media spotlight on politics and politically charged civic action. It is an arena that is misunderstood by many civic activists.

Despite the slogan that "the personal is political," personal ailments are generally treated as private matters, which get less respect and attention than public issues. A common attitude is that people talk about private woes; they act on public ones. For impatient Americans, talk is talk and action is action. For people seeking solutions to debilitating personal misfortune, however, talk is action. Comparing notes with other people whose internal turmoil has been slighted by others or is hidden from society is a powerful experience. "You feel like nobody else has gone through what you've been through, and you really need to talk about it," says a member of a support group for parents of children who died of a heart defect. Said another participant in the Healing Hearts discussions at Hackensack University Medical Center, "Part of it was just realizing that you weren't really crazy." By talking with other people enduring the same loss and pain, "you can kind of reason with yourself better," said a mother of a baby who died while waiting for a heart operation.

Consider another example of this phenomenon. After suffering from stuttering for decades, a distraught man in his fifties was facing elimination of his job as a newspaper typesetter because of computerized machinery. Desperate to be able to get through a job interview, the tongue-tied typesetter went to a speech therapist. When that treatment didn't work, he asked the therapist for the names of other stutterers. When they gathered at the typesetter's home and discovered they all had the same problem, these strangers talked and talked for hours and decided to meet every week to confront together their fear of speaking in public. From that gathering rose a mutual-help group for stutterers called Speak Easy. Its fifty-six-year-old founder enrolled in college and became a speech therapist helping kids who stutter, remembering how humiliated he had been by the punitive ways teachers in grade school had treated him.

Stories like this, which appeared in a 1998 *Bergen Record* profile of Speak Easy founder Bob Gathman of Paramus, are not uncommon in Garden State newspapers. One reason is that New Jersey hosts a national center for citizen groups dealing with personal-life problems. Since 1981, the New Jersey Self-Help Clearinghouse in Denville has aided the development of hundreds of mutual-aid groups focused on a multitude of serious conditions, from AIDS to multiple personality disorder to workaholism. In 1990 the program was expanded to provide a national networking service via the Internet and a frequently updated paperback directory that has become the bible of this grassroots citizens' movement.

"We help people not to reinvent the wheel," Edward Madara, the clearinghouse's founder and director, likes to say. Gatherings of mutual-help group members, for instance, can be very emotional. "In these meetings," says a member of a New Jersey group of World War II prisoners of war, "you hear a lot of yelling and screaming. That's good." It's good because for fifty years many of those war veterans didn't talk about their experiences, which haunted their nightmares. The intensity of such group encounters, however, can stress out organizers. What can be done to prevent emotional burnout? Madara's clearinghouse staff advises rotating the jobs of running meetings, handling telephone calls, and dealing with the public or the news media. "Keep in sight the fact that you are a member of a support group . . . people helping people. If you feel overburdened, or if you are concerned about a particular call, share your feelings with the other members of your group. That's what it's all about."

Such groups also find they are effecting positive change when members talk about their shared condition to the outside world. When members of such groups describe their experiences through newspaper accounts, TV shows, and talks to community groups and health professionals, more people gain insight and empathy for conditions they themselves were fortunate enough not to have encountered. Besides comforting their members, such groups "engage in education and actions and advocacy that have . . . often led to change in government and private institutional policies and programs," observed Alfred H. Katz, a UCLA professor emeritus of medicine, public health, and social welfare, in an insightful foreword to *The Self-Help Sourcebook*, a handbook published by Madara and clearinghouse supporters.

During the Vietnam War, I gained some insight into this process as a cofounder of a Vietnam veterans' rap group program in New York City that sought to address a problem that didn't fit the categories for treatment at Veterans Administration hospitals. Trying to cope with something that didn't meet the established definitions of war injuries, angry veterans who lived in New York, New Jersey, and Connecticut met around a conference table with several volunteer psychiatrists and psychologists. The veterans insisted that they were not there as patients but were seeking partners in probing a mystery that baffled the professionals. Otherwise healthy young men described living fractured lives years after coming home from Vietnam. "I was arguing with myself," one veteran said of a haunting dream. "Then there were two separate selves, and one of them finally shot the other, so I shot myself." What was different from shell shock, or the exhausted combat soldier's "thousand-yard stare," was that years went by before something triggered a delayed response to deadly events in people who thought they'd survived reasonably OK. The response could be so diffuse that even affected veterans didn't see the relationship to long-past events—until they heard others describe the same emotional turmoil, reveal similar nightmares, and discovered they weren't alone in feeling a little crazy and obsessed with things associated with Vietnam. "Post-Vietnam syndrome" was the tentative diagnosis suggested by Robert Jay Lifton, a Yale University psychiatry professor who had studied World War II atomic bombing survivors and treated Korean War combat veterans as an air force psychiatrist.

Out of those exploratory meetings of Vietnam veterans in New York as well as on the West Coast came the determination, the initial research, and the gaining of skills to pinpoint what subsequently came to be termed post-traumatic stress disorder. Several veterans enrolled in graduate school to gain professional credentials as psychologists and devoted their lives to work on this issue. Lifton and others wrote books about this phenomenon of veterans' rap groups challenging the established views of war's impact on survivors. As veterans active in this campaign compared notes, they realized that the experience was not unique to war veterans but also happened to other people who survived fires, car accidents, rape, or other traumatic events. Because of the work of these veterans' groups and the networking they did with others, post-traumatic stress disorder became an accepted war-related condition for VA medical treatment, and an officially listed psychiatric condition associated with trauma of all sorts, from childhood sexual abuse to doing rescue work at disaster scenes.

"Vietnam haunted me after I came home. But there was no place to go and no official place to turn. A group of us veterans, guided by Drs. Robert Jay Lifton, Florence Volkman-Pincus, and Chaim Shatan, created a model of a place to turn, to heal ourselves," recalled Jack Smith, a former marine sergeant who went from rap groups to graduate school and became founding director of the National Center for Stress Recovery, after helping set up a nationwide network of storefront clinics funded by the Veterans Administration to aid Vietnam veterans. He has also been a featured speaker at New Jersey Self-Help Clearinghouse workshops on recovery from traffic accidents. Smith, who helped write the American Psychiatric Association definition of post-traumatic stress disorder, emphasizes that people can help each other cope with the aftermath of a disaster, rather than rely on the myths that time heals all wounds and survivors shouldn't think about the past but should instead get on with their lives. What veterans of self-help groups have learned, Jack Smith conveys in a handbook on handling the often hidden damage from car accidents, is that "knowledge, understanding, and support all help people recover faster."

Rx: Public Advocacy

Advocacy by the afflicted that sparks public acknowledgment of an overlooked problem and pride in developing a mutual-assistance program creates a powerful medicine for individuals and society. One small group of Vietnam veterans upset by bitter postwar experiences launched the project in Washington, D.C., that created the Vietnam Veterans Memorial wall. Many veterans back from Vietnam had felt so disaffected at home that a disturbing number committed suicide. Others drank or drugged themselves to ease the combined pain of war memories and social rejection. Since its dedication in 1982, the somber wall on the Mall has become one of America's most visited sites, one where not only veterans mourn but millions of other Americans go as if to a shrine, to see and touch a wall of names dedicated not only to the dead of a distant war but also to the healing of a nation ripped apart by that war.

Another emotionally charged issue that many Vietnam veterans tackled was the gnawing suspicion that some lingering health problems were caused by the use in battle

zones of powerful herbicides, pesticides, and other potentially dangerous chemicals. The spraying of Agent Orange,
widely used to kill jungle vegetation, had been halted by
the federal government in 1971 after a scientific study found
a toxic component, dioxin, appeared to cause cancer, birth
defects, and higher-than-normal death rates in laboratory
animals. Some news reports noted similar health problems
appeared to have stricken some Vietnamese civilians exposed to herbicide spray. However, a host of U.S. agencies
including the Pentagon, Veterans Administration, and the
Environmental Protection Agency maintained there was no
proof that Agent Orange had harmed members of the American forces. Despite their differences on many other issues,
thousands of frustrated veterans got together and formed
regional, state, and national coalitions to research the issue
and promote health studies. In New Jersey, an ad hoc veterans coalition convinced the state legislature in 1980 to fund
an Agent Orange Commission to promote research into the
issue and prod federal agencies to cooperate in finding the
answer and accepting responsibility for caring for affected
veterans if these chemicals were found to have harmed
people's health. In 1992, a New Jersey Agent Orange Commission study found sperm and immune system abnormali-
ties in many Vietnam veterans. In 1993, a National Academy
of Sciences study linked three types of cancer, a liver disorder, and a severe skin disease to exposure to dioxin. Research
developed by the New Jersey Agent Orange Commission
that detected measurable levels of dioxin in veterans twenty
years after they returned from Vietnam was credited with
providing valuable information for the national study.

     In 1994, the New Jersey commission helped launch a
study of birth defects among children of Vietnam veterans.
In 1996, another National Academy of Sciences study found
a "limited or suggestive" link between exposure to the war-

time herbicide and a higher than average rate of spina bifida in children born to veterans who served in Vietnam. In the wake of that study, President Clinton asked Congress to grant disability payments to Vietnam veterans' children born with the spinal cord defect. The Veterans Administration announced that veterans who had any of seven diseases associated with dioxin exposure were now eligible for health care and disability payments.

When Vietnam veterans and other Americans first raised questions whether chemicals sprayed in Vietnam might have caused a rash of health ailments officials in Washington dismissed their concerns. The search for answers was pressed at the grassroots level. In a series of articles exploring the health questions about Agent Orange and other chemicals used in Vietnam, which a colleague and I wrote for the Morristown *Daily Record* in 1980, we interviewed dozens of veterans across the country. Many had conducted their own research into obscure scientific studies on chemical plant employees, farmers, and forestry workers in the United States and Europe that pointed to serious health effects from exposure to some of these herbicides. Some veterans had launched lawsuits against Agent Orange manufacturers in an effort to lay out in court evidence they felt was being ignored or covered up by the federal government. Others presented their findings to Congress and gained funding for a health study of Vietnam veterans to be done by a scientific agency. The pressure to find answers to these vexing questions finally overwhelmed the powerful forces that didn't want to pay for the consequences of earlier government decisions to drench the Vietnamese countryside and the people there, including GIs, with toxic chemicals.

"Vietnam vets were right all along," Congressman Lane Evans, a Democrat of Illinois, said when the Veterans Administration finally announced that it would treat veterans affected with cancer linked to exposure to Agent Orange. "For years, the government did not listen," President Clinton told Congress in seeking treatment for veterans' children with birth defects. "Today, we are showing that America can listen and act." By that time, the public had been soberly following the Agent Orange issue for years. Many community groups had been raising their own concerns about the manufacture and use of the same herbicides in American communities. In Newark, a former Agent Orange manufacturing plant became a Superfund cleanup site; scientists' studies showed the site had polluted the lower Passaic River so heavily with dioxin that it affected the safety of fishing and the dredging of ship channels for New Jersey's major seaports. In the wake of protests by community groups and environmental organizations, the substance that Pentagon officials had maintained was safe for soldiers was deemed by the Environmental Protection Agency to be too toxic to be moved to landfills from a sealed site in Newark or the muddy bottom of the Passaic River.

Other public education projects by people who share a common affliction and a commitment to soothing painful conditions have been no less emotionally powerful for the people who never saw a war zone. One of the most effective things members of a mutual-help group do is share painful stories, which both vent pent-up emotions and show each other how to cope with situations that others, including family members, don't understand. Indeed, the key to citizen action on personal-life issues is the public revealing of private stories about the anguish caused by an ailment many people don't take seriously and then showcasing the determined struggle to find solutions.

"Growing up, I wished I wasn't born," a Fair Lawn resident blurted to a newspaper reporter doing a profile of a mutual-aid group activist. "When you say 'learning disabilities,' people think you're stupid," said Randy Schwartz, who founded the Bergen County–based Coalition for Adults with Learning Disabilities after years of grappling with a mysterious malady that left him unable to tell left from right or write legibly. "Teachers would yell at me," said the forty-something professional photographer. "In sixth grade, I spent six months in the coatroom," ordered there by an exasperated teacher. In high school, he felt so isolated and unable to cope with academic work that he wanted to kill himself. "My parents didn't understand," Randy Schwartz recalled. Afraid to drive a car as an adult working in a battery factory, he went to a phobia resource center, where a counselor told him of a friend's son with a similar problem and urged him to undergo tests that pinpointed his disability.

He was thirty years old when he finally got a proper diagnosis of having dysgraphia. "There's no treatment, but there are compensating techniques," Schwartz learned. Finding out what the problem was and how to cope with it enabled him to earn a college degree in social work. "Now I feel a sense of hope and purpose. I'm trying to teach other adults with learning disabilities the same philosophy—to open up and share, so they can raise their consciousness and get rid of the embarrassment, shame, and self-hate."

The point of recounting Randy Schwartz's very personal story is to illustrate how people discover information vital to their lives, often after groping in the dark for years. It can be excruciatingly hard to find useful information without a forum focused on a particular problem. Creating such forums, as Randy Schwartz and Vietnam veterans concerned about their health problems and others have done, is not easy. As anyone who remembers grade school games knows, getting people to cooperate with each other is hard work. Harboring simmering social resentments from our youth, adults many times arrive at a meeting called to address a problem the group has in common suspicious of other people's agendas, ideas, behavior. Having helped spark numerous self-help groups, the staff at the New Jersey Self-Help Clearinghouse is alert to what often happens next.

"After a group is formed, changes can occur in a group's goals or purposes, leadership problems can spring up, difficult members can threaten the effectiveness of the group," they note in a notice on consultation services they offer. "Sometimes all that is needed is a handout of ideas for handling the specific problem; other times, more in-depth problem-solving is in order. Often, the best source of help for a troubled group is advice from another group."

Their down-to-earth advice, conveyed in a variety of how-to materials, starts with a suggestion to attend "one or more meetings of other self-help groups to get a feel for how they operate (especially if you're trailblazing and developing a new type of self-help group). Borrow or adapt what you consider good techniques to use in your own group." Clearinghouse materials cover how to reach out to other people to form a mutual-aid self-help group, organize informal and public meetings, set up phone networks, use professionals for advice and research assistance, listen to others and talk about one's own situation, deal with crisis calls, and prevent burnout.

"A calm voice can help calm a distraught caller," notes a section on handling a phone call from someone who sounds overwhelmed by his or her problems. Depending on the problem a self-help group is addressing, people who call a contact number for the group may feel suicidal or mad as hell that no one takes them or the problem seriously. "Gently acknowledge his/her feelings. . . . Let the caller know that it's all right that they are upset. . . . Helping the caller to feel more relaxed might enable him/her to explore with you other support networks, such as family, clergy, mental health centers, or friends. . . . Let the caller know that you understand and care. . . . Allow the caller to do most of the talking. . . . helping people to help themselves is not the same as rescuing. As a contact person, you are probably not trained in crisis intervention. You can listen to the person in crisis, and make referrals, but it is important to acknowledge your limitations."

There are techniques for running meetings that stay focused on the reason for the gathering. These include welcoming participants and briefly stating a proposed goal or goals, asking each person to introduce himself or herself and state his or her reason for coming to the meeting and what he or she would like to accomplish, writing down a list of topics participants want to discuss, and then going down the list. Future meetings can be focused on discussing in-depth one topic at a time, forming committees to work on various aspects from research to outreach, and hearing guest speakers—or a combination of these elements. The Clearinghouse has created useful how-to handouts on structuring group meetings.

No one, however, can provide advice on how people feel about each other. Every gathering of people has its own dynamic. You may find the group you joined or helped to form is not really for you. Other people's goals or methods or the way they deal with others may not be what you feel is the best way to do things. If it's not working for you, you are free to leave one group and join or start another one. Indeed, this is a grand American tradition, explaining in large part why there are so many various Protestant church denominations, so many towns in New Jersey, and an estimated half-million self-help groups across the United States.

Many times, one person or a handful of people decide they have a better vision than do the leaders of an established group, and they break off to form a new group.

Whatever the combination of participants, people have to get along with one another for a group to function effectively. In its most elemental form, this means: you talk, I listen; I talk, you listen. That's a hard thing for many people to do. It takes practice. "In a self-help group, the role of facilitating or leading a group discussion is not the sole responsibility of one person but the responsibility of the entire group," the Clearinghouse staff advises. Everyone should feel welcome to participate in discussions and should be listened to without interruptions or whispered asides.

Many groups manage the traffic control in emotional discussions by having a moderator and rotating that job. A good moderator notices when people don't speak and asks if they would like to comment. "What do you think?" is likely to entice the shyest person to respond. On the other hand, if someone doesn't want to talk, respect that. Some people are talkers, some are listeners. One value of self-help groups is hearing that other people have had the same experience, felt similar feelings, and are troubled by them, but are finding various ways to cope. Another value is saying how you feel to a group of people who don't put you down for revealing your private feelings and struggles to maintain an even keel amid an emotional and/or physical storm.

It's this sharing of experiences, feelings, and struggles to cope that gives people in a group validation of one's circumstances in life and a sense of hope that was hard, perhaps impossible, to find alone. Group meetings should provide a "supportive, caring, and non-judgmental atmosphere," the Clearinghouse staff emphasizes. This is much different than locker room talk or what goes on in many workplaces and at many family dinners, where comments to someone feeling blue can be cruel. "Allow a member to ventilate negative or angry feelings; often this must be done before positive advice can be given and received. Assure fellow members that whatever is said in the group stays there," adds a Clearinghouse handout on "Responsibility of Group Members to Each Other."

"It's much easier to start a group if the work is shared," says Madara, in an observation that applies to keeping an established group going. "But most importantly, if several people are involved in the initial work at that first meeting (publicity, refreshments, greeting new people, etc.), they will model for newcomers what your self-help mutual aid group is all about—not one person doing it all, but dependent upon the individual volunteer efforts and the active participation of all the other members." When meetings begin to attract fewer people than previously, he advises not to panic: "Expect your group to experience 'ups and downs' in terms of attendance and enthusiasm. It's natural and to be expected. You may want to consider joining or forming a coalition or state association of leaders from the same or similar groups, for periodic mutual support and the sharing of program ideas and successes."

The key to successful self-help groups is providing compelling local, regional, national, even international models of people addressing a serious problem in their lives, to show participants and other people that change is possible. To help people put together such groups, the New Jersey Self-Help Clearinghouse and its companion service, American Self-Help Clearinghouse, offer advice and assistance via telephone, mail, workshops, a handbook, an annual directory, and a Web site that lists contacts for thousands of self-help groups across the United States and Canada, and around the world. They provide guidance in establishing groups that meet in people's homes, larger settings such as churches and hospitals, or on-line via computer forum sites.

"Demonstration often is the best teacher," notes a section on "Starting an Online Self-Help Group" posted on the American Self-Help Clearinghouse Web site (www.cmhc. com/selfhelp/). In the computer age, the notion of what constitutes a support group can extend far beyond one's neighborhood or state or region. The data bank at the Clearinghouse offices in Denville lists more than four thousand self-help groups in New Jersey and more than eight hundred such groups in other states and countries. Check some of them out. Many offer specialized materials for forming a mutual-aid self-help group addressing a particular problem. Somewhere out there are other people who share your concerns. And if there is no group that addresses those concerns, you can start one. Thousands of people have done it.

Organizing Tips

1. Attend meetings of one or more self-help groups and note how they are conducted. Check out what's on the Internet.

2. If you are intent on forming a new group, seek out other people who might be interested and invite them to an organizing meeting. Get in touch with the New Jersey Self-Help Clearinghouse for contacts, advice, and to be listed on its Web site.

3. Publicize the meeting in local newspapers, church bulletins, library bulletin boards, social services agency newsletters, and other places that seem appropriate for reaching potentially interested people.

4. Form a speakers bureau to address community and other

groups about the goals of your group and how others can help.

5. Ask professionals in that field to serve on an advisory committee, speak at group meetings, guide members in doing research.

6. Undertake public education actions that convey what your group has learned about the situation it was formed to address, ranging from press interviews to lobbying to change laws or methods used by professionals.

5

Grassroots-to-

Global Civic

Action

The enemy looks like us and they are concerned about peace just like we are. My dream is that these "people-to-people" exchanges can help build an atmosphere of trust here as well as in the Soviet Union so that our leaders can come to some kind of agreement.

—Betty Jane Ricker, Montclair councilwoman, on return from citizen-exchange trip to the Soviet Union, October 1986

There is a saying in Russian: Drop by drop, we'll make a river . . . maybe we'll find an ocean of people to promote peace in the whole world.

—Izat Klychev, Soviet painter, on arrival in New York to visit New Jersey on citizen-exchange trip, March 1987

The times seemed desperate. The United States and the Soviet Union were squared off on opposing sides of regional and civil wars around the world. Talks on halting a new, potentially yet more devastating round of the nuclear arms race broke down when the United States government deployed its latest, exceedingly lethal nuclear-armed missiles in Western Europe aimed at Soviet military installations in Eastern Europe. Without warning, a Korean airliner that strayed over Soviet territory was shot down by a Soviet jet, killing all aboard, including a U.S. congressman. Amid these heightened tensions, a group of U.S. scientists issued a report that computer modeling of nuclear war warned that the smoke from massive fires could block sunlight for months, creating a "nuclear winter" that could be catastrophic for life on Earth. Without warning, a Soviet nuclear power station exploded, spewing radioactive clouds as far as Sweden. Weeks later, a Soviet physicist working at United Nations headquarters in New York was charged with being a spy, an American journalist in Moscow was accused of espionage, and the two feuding governments began expelling each other's diplomats from their capitals.

In the midst of this diplomatic meltdown, a delegation of New Jersey residents on a grassroots peace mission arrived in Moscow. The Soviet army was waging a war in Afghanistan against opponents supplied with weapons by the U.S. government. Peace movement organizers in the United States were being hounded by the FBI for making unauthorized contact with the enemy. The situation seemed to be yet another of the grim Cold War crises that had led to East-West blocs prepared to obliterate each other.

"When we left for the Soviet Union . . . other Americans were boycotting meetings with the Russians, our national governments were at loggerheads over the fates of two alleged spies, and the proposed summit meeting between Mr. Reagan and Mr. Gorbachev appeared to be in jeopardy," Montclair councilwoman Betty Jane (Bee Jai) Ricker, a member of the fourteen-person delegation sponsored by New Jersey civic groups, told the *Montclair Times* on her return. "Just a day before our Bridges for Peace delegation left Moscow, all these serious problems were reported to be resolved. I think, in a small but significant way, citizen exchanges such as ours help to create a better climate of trust between the USA and the Soviet Union, so that solutions to our differences can be found."

Perhaps the most important development of the late twentieth century was the geometric growth of a widespread citizens' campaign that aimed to prevent nuclear war. Sparked by escalating East-West clashes and U.S. civil defense preparations for waging nuclear war with the Soviet Union, millions of people in both nations undertook their own efforts to halt the lethal logic of Mutual Assured Destruction, the scorched-earth policy at the Pentagon and the Kremlin. Citizen groups across New Jersey, like those in many other places, conducted a series of campaigns in the 1980s to defuse the suicidal, hair-trigger targeting on both sides of thousands of missiles armed with thermonuclear devices with the power to destroy entire cities and, cumulatively, both nations.

One chilly day a Soviet delegation arrived in New Jersey. This was step two of the citizen-exchange project, just days after a prime-time television drama called *Amerika* aired, depicting a Soviet military occupation of the United States. As circumstances would have it, while these eleven Russian visitors were being greeted in numerous New Jersey communities—amid howls of outrage by the John Birch Society and other anticommunist groups—a boatload of Soviet sailors was rescued from a sinking freighter by U.S. Coast Guard helicopters and flown to a safe landing near Atlantic City. President Reagan promptly invited the Soviet crew and their rescuers to the White House.

"In the past, I've often talked about what would happen if ordinary Americans and people from the Soviet Union could get together, get together as human beings, as men and women who breathe the same air, share the same concerns about making life better for themselves and their children," Reagan told the Soviet seafarers, even as Soviet citizens invited by grassroots civic groups were being greeted in New Jersey towns and in other communities across the United States in that spring of 1987. "And here we have a case where just this happened. I hope and pray that no matter how stormy international affairs, the leaders of the world can look and see what happened . . . between these fliers and sailors, and be duly inspired. After all, this good planet whirling through space isn't very different from a ship upon the sea . . . We must reach out to each other in good will, for we have no other alternative," Reagan concluded, stating the case for making peace with the Soviet Union in uncharacteristically conciliatory remarks widely broadcast by the news media.

The next spring, Reagan traveled to Moscow and strolled through Red Square with Soviet Communist Party leader Mikhail Gorbachev, a historic peacemaking action that made official what was considered radical when citizen activists began such journeys to the Soviet Union. Reagan's embrace of Gorbachev and a nuclear-weapons reduction treaty signaled the end of the Cold War. This was an astonishing turnabout for a president who had painted the Soviets as evil personified, ordered military confrontation with the Soviet Union and its Third World allies in brushfire wars around the world, and accused the American peace movement of being part of a communist plot.

In an effort to pressure the fiercely anticommunist Reagan, who took office in 1981, to find diplomatic solutions to the flash points that threatened to ignite a war that could incinerate America and Russia, if not the entire world, an unusual coalition of peace activists and environmen-

talists, lawyers and doctors, municipal and state officials
was formed in New Jersey and other states to sponsor a ballot referendum asking voters if they would approve a mutual freeze on nuclear weapons in the United States and the
Soviet Union. On election day 1982, 66 percent of New Jersey voters favored such a diplomatic approach. Similar results were posted in seven other states and five major cities,
including Washington, D.C.

Despite this electoral message, nothing changed. Before
the vote, Reagan blasted the nuclear-freeze campaign as a
KGB plot. Fears that communism would undermine American ramparts hardened at the White House. Working within
the system and mobilizing large numbers of voters who expressed a preference for diplomacy over military confrontation had no more effect than had protest marches and civil
disobedience actions by peace groups that protested Reagan's
get-tough policy of declaring the Soviet Union an "evil em-
pire" and tightening the ring of nuclear missiles around its
borders. Given the Cold War mind-set that viewed peaceful
moves as an enemy plot and threats of war as national salvation, how could a ballot question transform decades of
hostility between two massively armed rival ideological
blocs?

Determined nuclear-freeze campaign organizers next
focused on intensive lobbying of Congress. Yet again, negotiations to curb the nuclear-arms rivalry were rejected. To
move the grassroots peace initiative from ballot question
and stymied lobbying to positive action, another citizens'
campaign arose. This one proposed to take the case for end-
ing the nuclear arms race to the people of the Soviet Union
by organizing citizen-exchange programs and creating sister-
city ties that would demonstrate that Americans and Russians could get along at the grassroots level. The aim of this
campaign, which launched an international phenomenon

dubbed "citizen diplomacy," was to challenge national leaders to follow suit. Within a few years, it was embraced by U.S. and Soviet leaders and played a crucial role in dismantling the Iron Curtain of bristling walls, barbed-wire fences, and doomsday armaments dividing Europe, and transforming Russia from a fearsome adversary into a trading partner.

How is it that citizen groups managed to break through barriers of fear and mistrust that confounded national leaders? What made this campaign so attractive to so many people is that it substituted cooperation for confrontation. This was an innovative antidote to the confrontation-charged atmosphere of the Cold War. To build bridges to the Soviets, organizers sought out a wide range of fellow citizens. In the bitter wake of the 1960s, however, Americans dealt with each other confrontationally. In order to form a broad-based grassroots coalition, citizen activists, religious figures, school and college officials, and other community leaders had to work hard to be diplomatic with each other, which provided good practice for dealing with the Soviets and demonstrating to the U.S. government what grassroots civic groups could accomplish.

Given the goal and conduct of this coalition, municipal officials in scores of American communities took the unprecedented step of aiding a citizens' peace campaign. This, it was soon discovered, provided crucial legitimacy in the Soviet Union for a campaign that purported to represent grassroots America to the Soviet people. Even as the Soviet Union tightened its borders against perceived military threats and kept U.S. diplomats and journalists confined to Moscow under close surveillance, that fortress nation cautiously opened its airports and train stations to an onslaught of American civic delegations who traveled to cities and villages across the country, bearing invitations to visit American communities and build "Bridges for Peace," as one of the many exchange groups called itself. Once assured, because they were conveyed in messages of greetings on official letterhead from mayors, municipal councils, public schools, churches, and other community organizations, that these invitations were genuine, the Kremlin allowed an outpouring of Soviet citizens to travel to America.

A key element in the citizen-exchange campaign is that this massive crossing of previously forbidding borders was not engineered by the warring governments, neither of which trusted anything the other did. It was organized, step by step, by civic groups frustrated by the failure of traditional diplomacy to halt the drift toward war between nations with the power to blow up the world. But before convincing people in the Soviet Union to help build bridges of peace spanning the abyss of nuclear war plans, Americans first had to convince one another to reach out to people long viewed in American society as our mortal enemies.

That sobering reexamination was sparked by a federal agency ordering municipal governments in the early 1980s to be prepared to follow nuclear war evacuation plans. From California to Colorado to New York and New Jersey, many residents and local officials protested that this was a thoughtless, dangerous directive. Many cities and towns countered this command by the Federal Emergency Management Agency by distributing locally produced public information booklets detailing the devastating impact nuclear warhead explosions would have on their communities, citing data published by other federal agencies, pointing out that there was no place to flee the tremendous blast and heat waves and radioactive fallout in the short time missiles could be launched and hit targeted areas. These booklets promoted prevention of such a disaster as the only realistic survival strategy.

"The better the people in two nations understand one

another, the less likely it is that their governments will misunderstand each other," argued a pamphlet titled "Nuclear War and Montclair: Is There a Place to Hide?" Mailed to every household in the Essex County community of 38,000 in January 1984, in the wake of similar booklets distributed in San Francisco; Boulder, Colorado; Cambridge, Massachusetts; and other cities, it advocated grassroots diplomacy through people-to-people exchanges and establishing a sister-city relationship with some community in the Soviet Union. The Montclair booklet was written by a citizens' committee, paid for by community fund-raising events, and mailed under the local YWCA's nonprofit permit. It included endorsements by Republican and Democratic members of the town council, the town manager in his role as civil defense director, and U.S. Senator Frank Lautenberg, one of the town's prominent residents. "I believe there can be no winner in a nuclear war," wrote Deputy Mayor James H. Ramsey in a statement similar to that made by local elected officials across the country. "The devastation would severely cripple, if not destroy, life as we know it. . . . Governments at all levels have an obligation to move us away from this possible destruction."

Most of these grassroots public information booklets urged support of the nuclear-freeze proposal and related negotiations with the Soviet Union. When the Reagan administration brushed aside the concerns of municipal and state officials and refused to join the Soviet Union in a moratorium on nuclear weapons tests or negotiate a freeze on the arms race, more and more elected officials in New Jersey and other states enlisted in the grassroots campaign to bury the hatchet with the Soviet Union.

In contrast to Vietnam War protests, when peace activists and government officials at all levels were usually on opposite sides, grassroots actions on preventing nuclear war thrived on cooperation among previously antagonistic groups. In Fort Lee one morning in 1984, an elderly lady with the local peace group paused outside the municipal building and laughed: "We're always fighting city hall. Now we're going inside and having a meeting with the mayor!" Inside, Mayor Nicholas Corbiscello ushered his visitors into his office and asked how he could help the nuclear-freeze committee. "I was one of the GI's who went into Nagasaki [after the atomic-bomb blast] in 1945," he said, as explanation for his embrace of a grassroots movement the president, a fellow Republican, had denounced.

Many other elected officials made dramatic gestures not only to embrace the grassroots peace movement but also to cloak it in the mantle of patriotism. In 1985, the Essex County Board of Freeholders, the legislative body of New Jersey's most populous county, unanimously approved a proposal to create a county peace agency, modeled on peace offices supported by city governments in Cambridge, Massachusetts, and Washington, D.C. The Essex County Office on Peace, which I directed from an office at home while also holding a public relations job with the national YWCA in New York City, published and distributed a booklet for county residents on how to help prevent nuclear war, helped to organize a state chapter of the US-USSR Bridges for Peace citizen-exchange program, and promoted the dedication of schools, municipal buildings, churches, YWCAs, and other gathering places as community Peace Sites, a campaign that began in New Jersey and quickly spread to other states and overseas.

On Veterans Day 1986, for instance, the Somerville Borough Hall was declared a Peace Site by the mayor and council. Mayor Emanuel R. Luftglass urged establishment of Peace Sites throughout New Jersey as a message to Washington and Moscow that Americans were serious about preventing nuclear war. To the applause of members of the local American Legion post, Somerville officials proposed sending a copy of their Peace Site resolution to Gorbachev, urging him "to ask towns in Russia to join with Somerville and declare government buildings as Peace Sites."

Even as Somerville's civic leaders were wondering how Russians would react to this call to create grassroots peace sites, residents of other New Jersey communities were preparing to host a delegation of Soviet citizens and hearing accounts of life in the Soviet Union from Garden State residents who had recently returned from a citizen exchange trip. Similar activities were taking place across the United States. In a groundswell of citizen diplomacy, civic groups and local officials in twelve hundred U.S. cities and towns contacted citizens and officials in Soviet cities and towns with messages of peace and proposals to foster steps to help prevent nuclear war. Through these contacts, sister-city ties began to be established. These included some surprising combinations, such as Trenton matched with the Lenin District of Moscow.

One day, high in the hills of Soviet Georgia, the New Jersey delegation that arrived in the U.S.S.R. amid the 1996 spy crisis was welcomed to a lunch stop in a vineyard on the outskirts of the tiny city of Telavi. "Do you know," the mayor of Telavi said through an interpreter, "that we have a sister city in America? Fort Collins, Colorado!" Despite the fact that at the time there were very few such relationships, such encounters demonstrated that it was possible to create connections with Soviet communities. As a member of that exploratory delegation, which went to Moscow and several other cities in Russia and two other Soviet republics, I carried a resolution of greetings and goodwill from the Essex County freeholders, a letter from the YWCA of the U.S.A. to the Soviet Women's Committee to confirm plans for an exchange of women civic leaders, and a request from Montclair civic groups to be matched with a Soviet community willing to explore a sister-city relationship. The delegation also carried an enormous "US-USSR Bridges for Peace" banner depicting a rainbow bridge linking an American urban skyline and onion-domed Russian towers. This banner, signed by dozens of groups and individuals who funded our trip, was displayed in every Soviet city and town we visited. Bee Jai Ricker conveyed a resolution of greetings from the Montclair Town Council. Other delegation members from throughout New Jersey brought greetings from their communities: Millville in Cumberland County, Princeton and Pennington in Mercer County, Basking Ridge in Somerset County, New Vernon in Morris County, Clifton and Pompton Lakes in Passaic County, Cresskill and Teaneck in Bergen County.

All our intensive preparations for arguing with snarling communists about why there should be peaceful relations after four decades of hostilities turned out to be less important than those letters of greetings. People in the Soviet Union, we found, needed no convincing about the dangers of nuclear war. They were eager for friendly interactions with Americans. Throughout our travels, we were accompanied by the sounds of our own stereotypes shattering around us. In Volgograd, we found that the tractor-manufacturing city that rose out of the ashes of Stalingrad already had twelve sister cities around the world, including Coventry, England, and Hiroshima, Japan—two other cities devastated in World War II. Its officials and civic groups were eager to be matched with a U.S. city. While they anticipated being officially matched with Cleveland, Ohio, or some other industrial city in the American Midwest, our visit launched an unofficial relationship between the Volgograd region and

New Jersey that blossomed into student and teacher exchanges, and business and professional ties.

Organizing Strangers in an International Campaign

Getting people who don't know each other, who live in widely separated communities, to work together on a joint campaign is the ultimate test of an idea—and its advocates. The United States nearly split apart after winning its revolution against the British because, in drafting a constitution, small states like New Jersey didn't trust large states like Virginia to share national power. It took a compromise brokered by Benjamin Franklin to create the government of shared, balanced powers that Americans today take for granted. People generally are fiercely protective of their turf and eye other groups suspiciously. So organizing strangers to work cooperatively with people who live in another place requires perhaps more sophisticated skills than does organizing friends and neighbors to do a community project.

The principle is the same, however. The key ingredient, besides a compelling idea, is effective networking. Skilled organizers of statewide, national, and international campaigns recruit people who have good community credentials and ask them to organize within their community, social, religious, educational, professional, and other networks (such as veterans' groups). They are asked to reach out to people likely to listen to them about the merits of a new or expanding campaign tackling an issue that might seem overwhelming for an individual to try to address.

That's how the idea of citizen diplomacy to the Soviet Union came to New Jersey. A man from Vermont knew the minister of a church in Montclair. The minister hosted for his old acquaintance an informal gathering of local peace activists to hear about a small New England–based organization with a big idea that wanted to expand its base of operations. The idea was succinctly conveyed in the organization's name: US-USSR Bridges for Peace. The visitor from Vermont, Clinton Gardner, explained in a low-key, businesslike way that he was a businessman and World War II veteran who had become frustrated with the inability of the nuclear-freeze campaign to stop the saber-rattling that had become American policy toward the Soviet Union. So he and a small circle of like-minded New Englanders organized several exchanges between civic and religious groups in Vermont and neighboring states and the Soviet Peace Committee and Russian Orthodox Church. The Soviet government, he noted, was paranoid about spies and military incursions. It loathed religious groups smuggling Bibles into the officially atheist nation or making a human rights issue of its treatment of Jews who wanted to emigrate. Nonetheless, it seemed receptive to exchanges of a wide spectrum of citizens on both sides. Gardner had developed contacts for future exchanges. And he had worked out an affordable fund-raising budget for community groups willing to send representatives on small delegations to the U.S.S.R. for two weeks and, in return, host several Russian visitors for a portion of a two-week trip to the United States.

Having been carefully developed and concisely presented to a group of peace activists, it was an idea that virtually sold itself. Even so, to raise the money needed for an initial two-year exchange project and have the widest public impact, it had to be conveyed to people across the state of New Jersey. This would mean convincing leaders of existing peace coalitions, including the nuclear-freeze campaign, to accept a new project. To broaden the Bridges for Peace appeal, the idea was also presented to religious groups, schools and col-

leges, and municipal governments. Meetings with potentially interested parties were held in various sites. At one
meeting at a church in Princeton, I wrote these notes of the
animated brainstorming discussion that took place among
people from various parts of the state: "Cooperation, community, citizen, circles. . . . Widening circles, community
to community, citizen to citizen."

That, in a nutshell, is how this campaign was organized.
It expanded upon the model provided by Gardner, which he
subsequently laid out in a book, *Building Bridges: US-USSR;
A Handbook for Citizen Diplomats*, published in 1989. Besides the details of what to pack for a trip behind the Iron
Curtain and how to host Soviet visitors to American communities without exhausting them with nonstop activities,
the book's photos and descriptions of several exchanges
showed that it could be done and the exciting impact it had
on participants and Soviet-American relations.

"Four years ago when I joined with American and Soviet friends to found the US-USSR Bridges for Peace project,
only a wild optimist could have imagined the progress that
citizen diplomacy had made by 1987," Gardner wrote in an
article published in *New Times*, a Soviet foreign affairs
weekly, reprinted in the handbook he edited. "Then there
were a handful of organizations sponsoring Soviet-American exchanges. Now there are hundreds. Then Americans
who invited Soviets into their homes had to defend their
loyalty; now the Reagan administration announces that citizen exchanges are a pillar of its Soviet policy."

In another reprinted *New Times* article, one of the
newspaper's top editors, Alexander Pumpyansky, offered his
reflections on a March 1987 visit to America. "How warm
was the reception we were accorded in New Jersey!" he
wrote. The Soviet delegation was "welcomed as representatives of what was for [Americans] a newly discovered country."

In town after town, he found, Soviet visitors were objects of fascination and were peppered with questions about their lives and views on America.

Creative Communications

One of the most impressive things about New Jersey, Pumpyansky wrote, were church walls displaying posters showing photos of Soviet men, women, and children at work and play, with captions taken from a poem by Wendell Berry, "To a Siberian Woodsman." Among the lines Pumpyansky quoted for Soviet readers: "Who has invented our enmity? Who has prescribed us hatred of each other? Who has armed us against each other with the death of the world?" These lines of poetry accompanying photos of the "enemy" were printed on posters by the Fellowship of Reconciliation and hung in many churches and community centers during the 1980s. In this creative grassroots communication, using eye-catching photos and memorable poetry, Pumpyansky saw an American society wrestling with its role in the Cold War, a phenomenon that had been hidden by the acrid smoke of partisan volleys that permeated the news media in both nations. "If the underlying idea of Bridges for Peace were capsuled in a single line," he wrote, quoting again from Wendell Berry, "it would read thus: 'Let us look into each other's eyes, let us visit each other, talk and work together.'"

As these examples from the Bridges for Peace handbook illustrate, effective citizen campaigns create their own ways of communicating with the public. They don't rely on the news media to convey their concerns. In this case, circumstances also attracted news media attention to this project. Given the 66 percent favorable vote by New Jersey voters for the nuclear-freeze initiative, the state's news media treated the Bridges for Peace campaign as important news. Even so, to make certain that campaign goals were presented clearly and campaign actions reported accurately, much attention was paid to issuing timely press releases that conveyed the facts of who, what, where, when, and why—bolstered by quotable statements by key participants.

To demonstrate how much this was a grassroots campaign, multiple spokesmen and spokeswomen were presented and the diversity of participants highlighted. Among the fourteen men and women visiting the Soviet Union on the exchange trip were a public school teacher, a Catholic school teacher, a Presbyterian minister, a Methodist minister, an Episcopal Church representative, a Quaker peace activist, a Jewish peace activist, a black civil rights activist, a hospital administrator, a banker/Vietnam veteran, a writer/Vietnam veteran, a housewife, and a widowed senior citizen. Sponsoring groups included Bergen County SANE/Freeze; Coalition for Nuclear Disarmament in Princeton; Episcopal Diocese of New Jersey; Essex County Office on Peace; New Jersey SANE; Passaic County Nuclear Freeze Coalition; Union Congregational Church of Montclair; United Methodist Conference of Southern New Jersey; and World Peacemakers, Northern New Jersey Branch, based in Morristown.

Profiles of those going to the Soviet Union on a peace mission were offered to hometown newspapers, which were eager to cover this hot international issue from a local angle. Upon coming home, participants wrote accounts of their experiences in the Soviet Union, which appeared in a wide variety of publications. As one of the exchange participants, I presented, for instance, a travel section interview to the Newark *Star-Ledger*. I also wrote an issues-oriented article for a Paterson-based lawyers' journal, provided a press release to the *Montclair Times* conveying comments by three town residents on the Bridges for Peace delegation, and wrote an activist-oriented account for the newsletter of New Jersey SANE, one of the prime sponsors of the project. Many of the participants gave television and radio interviews. That was just part of our public outreach regarding this campaign. Color slides and videotape taken during fascinating encounters with people in the Soviet Union were used in presentations to church, school, and civic groups. A great deal of person-to-person conversation took place to line up hosts and sponsors of events for the Soviet delegation coming to New Jersey in the spring. The arrival of the Soviet visitors sparked another round of media coverage, articles by participants, and outreach to more churches, schools, and civic groups to plan another round of exchange visits.

How is it possible for people who are volunteers, with workplace and family responsibilities, to manage a complex project such as a citizen-exchange campaign? The secret ingredient: organize a coalition of many groups. Coordination and implementation of the New Jersey Bridges for Peace campaign was parceled out among many participants. Committees of people who lived near each other and the groups they networked with took responsibility for various aspects of this project, which included: raise more than $25,000 to send a delegation to the Soviet Union and host Soviet visitors, present a conference at Princeton University on citizen diplomacy during the Soviets' stay, treat the guests to tours of New York City and Trenton, line up schools and community events for them to visit, put them up in people's homes in a number of towns, and get all members of the group to where they were to be on a tight, two-week schedule that spanned the length and breadth of New Jersey.

The fund-raising was spread among several groups; each was responsible for raising a $1,700 portion of total expenses, plus $925 air fare for the representative who traveled to the Soviet Union. These amounts could be readily raised through modest community fund-raising events, such as bon voyage parties. An innovative idea that raised a substantial amount of money was selling for $10 each signature slips that were glued onto the Bridges for Peace banner, forming the arch of the bridge. The conference at Princeton University's Woodrow Wilson School of Public and International Affairs, called "Creating a World Beyond Stereotypes: A US-USSR Dialogue," was organized by Princeton-area residents with ties to the university. It was open to the public, for a $15 registration fee to cover expenses including lunch. One hundred people signed up. The conference provided American and Soviet keynote speakers and workshops where small groups of Americans and Soviet visitors addressed divisive Soviet-American issues ranging from military threats to religion and politics. The Saturday event, as advertised in the promotional flier, was designed "to bring together citizens of both countries in a peaceful environment, to meet one another face to face, and to reach beyond the rhetoric which tends to characterize our understanding of each other's country." It attracted a picket line of anticommunist hard-liners, a variety of New Jerseyans curious to talk with real live Russians, and a flurry of news media attention. The tour of Trenton was organized by people with State House ties and required little in the way of a budget beyond lunch at a historic tavern. The tour of Manhattan, which included a stay in a midtown hotel, was scheduled for the day before the Soviet delegation departed from Kennedy International Airport. A rented bus did double duty to get them to the airport on time after a day of sightseeing and shopping.

Finding volunteers willing to host a Soviet guest or two in their home for a night or two or drive them from one place to another was the easiest part of organizing this project. Lots of people wanted an opportunity to spend some time talking with Russians, to reassure them that Americans did not want to wage a nuclear war. "In Paterson," Alexander Pumpyansky wrote in a *New Times* article on his travels in New Jersey, "we stayed (together with . . . Olimpiada Butina, a worker at a Leningrad sweet factory, member of the parliament of the Russian Federation, mother of twins, expecting to be a grandmother at any minute, on her first visit to America) with Marjory and Jim Bains. . . . We saw Jim [a William Paterson College professor] only early in the morning at breakfast or late in the evening when we returned from the various discussions and meetings. Marjory organized some of these discussions and so we spent quite a lot of time together. Good-humoured, always ready to joke at her own expense or about circumstances, she was our invariable companion on the Paterson route—our hostess, driver and guide."

In Hopewell, Pumpyansky was hosted by Anne and Dale Bussis. The stranger from Moscow was amazed when his hostess told him as he went out to an event that "if you get back before us, you'll find the side door open." He learned that these "two elderly but absolutely indefatigable people" had raised six adopted children and that Dale was just back from Nicaragua, where he had helped build homes with a Habitat for Humanity project. From such encounters, Pumpyansky concluded, "What I like about the American peace organizations . . . is that their actions are concrete and their thinking is in terms of humanity as a whole."

Working in such a campaign was exciting and emotionally exhausting. To prepare to help coordinate this project, I attended a conference in Massachusetts when that state's Bridges project hosted Soviet visitors in the spring of 1986. Using the Massachusetts project as a guide, we made adjustments to fit circumstances in New Jersey. Given the length of the state and diversity of participating groups, two of us shared co-coordinator roles. Patricia Compton, who lived near Princeton and represented the Trenton-based Episcopal Diocese, oversaw project organizing in central and southern New Jersey. I focused on North Jersey groups and scheduling. In addition to our frequent telephone conversations, representatives of all the groups that sponsored our state project held periodic meetings. Committees or teams of sponsoring groups took responsibility for various matters. Despite our diverse backgrounds, everyone deferred to each other's turns of leadership—hosting a planning meeting, moderating a public event, making phone calls to coordinate activities, giving a press interview—in a cooperative, consensus-based alliance forged by the utter seriousness of the issue.

Clint Gardner and Richard Hough-Ross also provided experienced guidance. The president and executive director, respectively, of US-USSR Bridges for Peace, they traveled frequently from Vermont to New Jersey to keep us on track to get passports, visas, and airline tickets, and prepare us to enter the mysterious Soviet Union during a frosty time in Soviet-American relations. They emphasized that we had to prepare ourselves thoroughly, to become familiar not only with the controversial nuclear-weapons issues but also with Russian and Soviet history, some Russian language phrases and the Cyrillic alphabet, the status of religion in the Soviet Union, and the diversity of its ethnic groups and republics. They provided concisely focused study materials and workshops that I felt prepared us to go to the Soviet Union as "peace champions" (as one Soviet newspaper called us) far better than the United States Army prepared me to go to Vietnam as a soldier. When we went to the Soviet Union, Clint accompanied our New Jersey group, while Richard accompanied a group of religious representatives who were hosted by the Russian Orthodox Church and Russian Baptist churches. As we traveled by plane, train, and bus around the Soviet Union, our two groups crossed paths with each other and encountered other Americans—businessmen, students, lawyers taking a look at the Soviet legal system, some tourists, blithely traveling in Russia amid a spy crisis.

Given the nature of our mission, we were welcomed in unexpected places far from Moscow, such as a massive tractor factory in Volgograd that had made tanks in World War II and a tiny synagogue on a back street in Tbilisi, Georgia, where U.S. diplomats, journalists, and tourists seldom if ever had been. To my surprise, no one in the Soviet Union directed any hostility toward me as a Vietnam War veteran. Instead, Soviet war veterans and other citizens shared their views about Soviet military involvement in Afghanistan. Some defended that war policy; others called it "Russia's Vietnam." Several of the people we met in Moscow and other Soviet cities made the point that in the nuclear age we faced two choices: to live together or to die together. "We can discuss human rights, Afghanistan, Cuba, Central America, whatever you want. Only on one condition—that we are alive," said one of our hosts, a chain-smoking former diplomat. "It is not enough to say we are both nice people. We have to work for disarmament, or we may not have an opportunity to solve any other problems."

As a result of the groundwork laid in that first round of citizen exchanges, a new world of possibilities opened up. High school students and teachers were exchanged. Ramapo College of New Jersey developed an exchange program with a university in Volgograd, gaining a Russian-language instructor and sending students to study for a semester in Russia. New Jersey businesses developed customers in the Soviet Union. "A sizable portion of our business is exports to Russia," the owner of a Clifton company that manufactures sausage-making machines told a group of visitors from Russia, who had come to see their new sister city of Montclair, in December 1992. The Russians got a tour of the sausage equipment plant as part of a two-week "cram course in capitalism" provided by Montclair State College and several New Jersey businesses. With the dissolution of the Soviet Union, the Russians were interested in American business methods and products. "We would like to supply our farmers with models for processing food, so food will not be lost" in the antiquated Soviet system, said Yuri E. Moshkin, deputy mayor of Cherepovets, a city of three hundred thousand people in northern Russia.

After hosting several Soviet peace delegations and highlighting its experiences with sister cities in England, Austria, and Nicaragua, Montclair was matched with the industrial city of Cherepovets. At first glance, a midwestern smokestack city would seem to have been a better match. But Montclair's suburban business community, town and school officials, and state university were delighted to be asked to help a smoggy, rusty steel-manufacturing center make the transition from Soviet life to a new Russian future. And residents of both communities appreciated that they were helping to make history.

Arriving in Montclair in July 1991 at the head of the first group of visitors from the new sister city, the mayor of Cherepovets, Vyacheslav R. Pozgalev, announced to his hosts that he had been an officer in the Soviet strategic missile force. "In the middle of dinner, Pozgalev put down his silverware and pointed at me from across the table and said, 'Last year, my missiles were aimed at you,'" Linda Wanat, Montclair's town clerk, recalled in a 1998 *Montclair Times* retrospective on the community's sister-cities' programs, which were started in the aftermath of World War II. "Then

I replied, 'As a child, I thought all Russians had horns and a tail.' At that point, we toasted our friendship and these new perceptions. We were thought to be enemies, and then we were sharing dinner." During that visit, the recently elected mayor told a *Montclair Times* reporter that soldiers at his missile station used to joke "that they should call up American soldiers at U.S. missile sites, and suggest they all go out to the movies together. 'If we will understand each other, war will never happen,'" Pozgalev said.

Such stories are also part of how citizen campaigns work. What the mayor of a city deep in Russia, who had been part of the military force we feared, had to say to Americans was not reported on national television. A citizen-exchange project provided the opportunity, and the forum, for this former Soviet Army officer to talk about making peace. Through such exchanges, residents of communities across America heard first-hand or read in local newspapers what representatives of the "enemy" had to say for themselves. Soviet citizens heard what Americans had to say, unfiltered by the foreign policy mesh that constrains both nations' national news media. When lots of these grassroots exchanges took place, Soviet-American relations shifted from frosty to friendly in a remarkably short time.

When a handful of Montclair residents suggested in 1983 that a solution to the nuclear arms race was to develop a sister city in the Soviet Union, the mayor and town council expressed support but made it clear such a project should be pursued unofficially by concerned residents. Worried about the threat of nuclear war but not wanting to appear too radical, the Republican mayor and council majority declined to provide taxpayer funds to print a booklet about how citizens could help defuse the danger of nuclear war. As individuals, however, they helped muster community support for that project and subsequent citizen-exchange programs. On this issue, they deferred the lead to citizen activists, whose role clearly was to test uncharted waters of public opinion.

This exploration expanded the realm of possibilities for many Americans. Once the idea of fostering citizen exchanges with the Soviet Union was floated in public, it grew far beyond the circle of peace activists who proposed it. It was championed by the Essex County freeholders, who sent a resolution to Moscow and hosted the first Soviet exchange group to visit New Jersey. It was lauded in newspaper editorials—and denounced as dangerously naive in others. It was embraced by Ramapo College administrators, who signed on with US-USSR Bridges for Peace to help develop the New Jersey–Volgograd relationship. It drew the support of several community and regional religious organizations and the business-oriented Rotary International clubs that sponsor international student exchanges. It sparked the idea of doing business with Russians.

After numerous attempts to get a match through Sister Cities International failed, Montclair's once seemingly quixotic quest was brought to fruition by Juliana Belcsak, a leader of Overseas Neighbors, a civic group that has sponsored a sister-city link between Montclair and Graz, Austria, since 1950. Belcsak, who runs an international business consulting firm, met some Russians at an international trade conference and pressed the idea further. She badgered agencies in Washington and Moscow. When a match was announced, she called upon the expertise of community groups such as Overseas Neighbors and Rotary not only to host visiting dignitaries and exchange students and teachers but also to provide medical assistance to seriously ill Russian children needing expensive operations, and business advice for creators of a new economic way of life.

"The people of Cherepovets have put an awful lot of

hope and faith in us," Belcsak wrote supporters of the sister-city project in March 1998, announcing the latest visit by a delegation from the Russian city, now struggling in a faltering Russian economy. "They still can't believe that we are all volunteers and that we really mean to make it a better world through our people-to-people programs. They have already come a long way since we first became 'friends' but there are still incredible problems in Cherepovets, but also marvelous opportunities for us to show them what we can do."

When it comes to economic issues, Americans may not have all the answers. But helping Russians address economic problems is a long way from trying to figure out how to counter Soviet nuclear-armed missiles. That the issues have changed so dramatically in a few years is testament to the efforts of grassroots citizen-exchange programs that turned Russians from deadly adversaries into partners in solving the problems of peace.

Organizing Tips

1. Parcel a complex campaign into committee-size parts.
2. Use multiple leadership, with a different person or committee in charge of each step. Select a campaign coordinator or, if covering a wide geography, co-coordinators. This person or team must be good at delegating responsibilities and keeping tabs on numerous activities, and enjoy working with diverse groups of people.
3. Develop a coalition of groups, with major decisions made by consensus of representatives of the member groups.
4. Spread fund-raising over a number of groups, so no single group has a large goal to reach.
5. Present several articulate spokespersons to the news me-

dia and in a speakers' bureau, providing a diversity of voices promoting the project.

6. Stretch the coalition's outreach as widely as possible. Support may well be found, by asking, in surprising quarters.

7. Keep the focus on cooperation, not confrontation; issues, not personalities. Citizen campaigns have clout when they attract lots of people to do something voluntarily for the cause. They lose clout fast when they tackle a government official or agency and nothing changes. The goal of a civic campaign is to accomplish something with citizen action that challenges or invites government officials to do likewise.

8. Determine whether the campaign's goal is met when circumstances change for the better, or whether some institutionalization is needed to maintain that new climate.

6

Putting It

All Together

Every effective civic campaign starts with a vision. The basic ingredient in any worthwhile grassroots campaign is believing that its goal can be achieved. Without faith that a project can be accomplished, all the skills in the world won't make it happen. On the other hand, faith can't build a house without carpentry skills, or mobilize people without people skills. So where do you find what you need to know after you've decided something needs to be done? Start with some research. Check the public library, the Internet. Look for books and newspaper and magazine articles about the issue you're concerned about. Look into organizations addressing that issue. Look for models of what you think should be done. Discuss this issue and what might be done about it with friends, family members, neighbors, coworkers, fellow students, teachers, alumni at your school or college. Somebody else may have a better idea.

How far a civic campaign will go depends on a lot of people. Your first priority is to figure out where you can best fit into a group of busy people. Are you launching a new project? Joining an ongoing one? In either case, there are many roles that need to be filled. One of the most important roles is recruiting volunteers and matching them to work that needs doing. In any campaign, there are technical aspects, such as how to publish a newsletter or create a Web site, and political/social aspects—how to convince other people to support the cause. There are also administrative, fund-raising, and public relations needs. Unless you're a one-person dynamo and can juggle multiple roles, choose an area you feel most comfortable with and master that. Coordinate what you are doing with other people in the campaign. Ask other people for advice. Many people are delighted to share what they've learned from experience. If there is a similar project you can visit, go take a look. Take note of interesting ideas.

Be aware that civic groups are no more immune than the rest of society from incompetence, fraud, or other ways of wasting funds and hardworking people's time. Check things out. Ask questions. Before investing your time and money in any civic campaign, be a savvy shopper. Too often, volunteers act as though doing something for society means being idealistic—and acting idealistic means leaving one's critical faculties and common sense at home. Here's how one writer described retirees who do volunteer work: "Even people who are skeptical of the value of their assignments stick with them. Sometimes it doesn't seem to matter what they are doing, just as long as they are *doing* . . . with few exceptions these activities bear little relation to their previous careers and require little or no expertise," wrote columnist Betty Weir Alderson in *Remedy* magazine. That description is hardly a prescription for an effective citizen campaign.

A serious civic activist marshals everything he or she has learned from previous experience that can help advance the cause. An effective organizer constantly seeks efficient ways to use limited time to do lots of things. "When my children, Sue, Karl and Mark, get together, they often recall that the only way they were permitted to watch television was if they folded, stuffed and licked envelopes for mailings," Helen Fenske recalled of her years as a housewife-turned-conservationist helping to coordinate the campaign to save the Great Swamp. "Most often, Art was left to supervise the operation," she said of her husband, a business executive, while she dashed to press the issue at community meetings.

When a lobbying campaign was needed to gain wilderness protection status for the swamp from Congress, Fenske and other Great Swamp activists mobilized members of garden clubs across America. These were largely mothers experienced at juggling domestic duties and civic improvements, and they could relate to saving a little piece of nature in New Jersey. At the time, conservation organizations were mainly run by men, who focused on large tracts of wilderness such as the Adirondacks. A male lobbyist for the Wilderness Society provided the garden clubs with a "stepladder" list of House and Senate committees and sequence of votes a proposed bill had to navigate.

"As each step was passed, those Garden Club ladies throughout the country would again tackle their congressmen with letters and personal contacts to address the next step in the passage of this legislation. The result was that in every state its congressional representatives were repeatedly contacted by hundreds of women from within their congressman's own constituency base. To this day, I marvel at the fierceness of their commitment and their effectiveness," Fenske recalled at a Great Swamp Watershed Association dinner honoring her conservation career. "If I ever wanted to start another national campaign, believe me, my first stop would be the Garden Club of America. That organization is totally underestimated in terms of its effectiveness when it takes up a cause!"

Well-organized civic campaigns often succeed because their opponents underestimated them. Grassroots activists, however, need to be wary of arrogant boasting, which can alienate people if an underdog starts sounding like a swaggering Goliath. The most compelling element of an effective citizens' campaign is low-key leadership that exhibits hardworking, selfless competence. Accomplished organizers turn the spotlight on others' accomplishments, both to share the accolades and to show the public the width and depth of the campaign.

Some nonprofit organizations teach leadership, lobbying, organizing, and other elements of civic activism. The Community Foundation of New Jersey in Morristown, for example, offers a training program, called Neighborhood Leadership Initiative, for community organizers. The New Jersey Sierra Club in Princeton offers environmental campaign workshops, training manuals, and a how-to Action Center on its Web site. New Jersey Peace Action in Montclair and the Fellowship of Reconciliation in Nyack, New York, offer workshops and training materials on international conflict resolution. The War Resisters League in New York City and Training for Change in Philadelphia provide workshops and materials on civil disobedience and other nonviolent acts of peace activism. In various cities, Habitat for Humanity provides workshops and how-to brochures on building houses and better neighborhoods.

Some colleges have begun to address the need for teaching community action organizing. Rutgers University has developed a Citizenship and Service Education (CASE) program that offers a combination of courses and coordinated placement in community projects. Ramapo College in Mahwah has hosted annual environmental conferences that bring together environmental activists, environmental agency officials, and eco-business entrepreneurs to exchange ideas and project successes.

Most citizen campaigns are informal—sign up as a volunteer and get on-the-job training. The competency of that training can range from excellent to abysmal. Many campaigns are launched by people with no previous experience of organizing people for cooperative action. Basically, they recruit friends and relatives and ask them to take charge of publicity, fund-raising, or other elements of a grassroots campaign. This is somewhat like enticing people to learn to swim by throwing them into deep water. Lots of people recoil from such an introduction to activism because they feel they're in over their heads. As with learning to swim, civic activism preferably should be practiced with an experienced guide. Whether you are joining an existing civic campaign or launching one, there are some basic elements it would be prudent to learn.

Civic campaigns, like military ones, deploy people using various tactics (short-term actions) and strategies (long-range plans). The analogy to war, however, should stop there. Civic campaigns are about improving communities, not assaulting them—or destroying the town to save it, to paraphrase a U.S. Army officer describing a bombed-out village in Vietnam. What began as a "civic action" nation-building strategy of winning over Vietnamese villagers was turned by military tactics into "WHAM," a sardonic GI acronym for the tragic "winning hearts and minds" slogan. Civic campaigners who intend to avoid the same fate should aim at gaining supporters from all sides, not going after enemies, real or imagined.

The common ingredient in successful citizens' campaigns is the strategic deployment of appropriate tactics. These include:

- *Framing the issue*: Concisely state the problem and proposed solution.
- *Demonstrating change*: Provide a model of the campaign's proposed solution. Point out precedents, create a small version of the larger goal.
- *Leadership by example*: Build the model and show others how to follow suit.
- *Networking*: Reach out to work with wider and wider circles of other groups.
- *Lobbying*: Seek support of government officials, at all levels, in public meetings and private talks.
- *Speaking*: Utilize a speakers' bureau to do outreach to community, school, religious, and other groups.
- *Writing*: Raise the issue and campaign's goal in letters, leaflets, letters to editors, press releases, newsletters, booklets, Internet postings.
- *Protest actions*: Marches, picket lines, civil disobedience.

While good as a tactic for raising an issue, protest actions may be the least effective in effecting a solution— unless combined with a host of other tactics aimed to bring about desired change, not just offer moral witness. "The experiences of the civil rights movement are still a very strong influence on organizers today. Unfortunately, many of the tactics that had great success in the 1960s are no longer effective in most situations," noted Si Kahn, author of two books on lessons from community organizing in the American South. "The cold hard fact is that marches and picket lines don't scare anyone any more unless they represent and are a symbol for other types of power," he wrote in *How People Get Power*, a primer on grassroots organizing.

In *Organizing: A Guide for Grassroots Leaders*, the comprehensive work he is most noted for, Kahn warns of relying on strategies and tactics that worked for some past campaign. "Good strategy is best made through wide-open thinking—when people follow their instincts, their hunches, their crazy ideas. Good strategists are always asking, 'What if we do something really different this time?'" He counsels citizen groups to keep a flexible strategy and be willing to change it when an approach is not working. "If the strategy we use to fight an issue either alienates people or fails to involve them, we'll find ourselves without the members that are necessary to win at all." Kahn's sensible counsel, developed from decades as a civil rights, union, and community organizer, is, regrettably, seldom related to specific cases. It's hard to tell from his repertoire of organizing advice what may work in which circumstances.

Reading and asking veteran organizers about previous campaigns can provide useful ideas. It can also point up pitfalls. Look critically at historic examples. For instance, some tactics of the 1960s peace movement boomeranged. Instead of working to change war supporters' minds, many groups used protest actions, such as burning draft board documents or the U.S. flag, that alienated millions of Americans. Antiwar coalitions mounted picket lines, marches, and a barrage of civil disobedience protests as a power tactic against a government waging war. Such tactics, borrowed from the civil rights movement and union campaigns, did not stop the Vietnam War. They infuriated people who had sons and neighbors fighting in Vietnam. They attacked the very entity—traditional patriots and their representatives in Congress—who had the power to end the war. Funds for military action in Vietnam were cut off when those groups eventually questioned the war's costs. Tragically, that came after more than a decade of destruction that tore Southeast Asia apart and years of polarizing protest actions that tore

America apart. Much of the lingering bitterness stemming from the sixties has to do with antiwar tactics that alienated people instead of educating and mobilizing them to save their sons and neighbors and residents of war-torn Asia.

In contrast, a cooperative rather than confrontational campaign helped end the Cold War threat of nuclear war. Tactics in that campaign had to bridge polarized positions and create mutually supporting actions by activist groups and government agencies, because protesting a nuclear war would have been too late. Since prevention was the solution, U.S. government officials, anticommunist Americans, Soviet citizens, and Communist Party officials had to be included in order for the campaign to succeed. In addressing an issue, focus on what actions and coalitions are needed to change the political and social climate to support your campaign's proposed solution.

Besides organizational tactics and strategy, activists need personal ones. While keeping an eye on what's good for the group's cause, keep the other eye on what you realistically can do. Chances are the campaign you are involved in will not attain its goal in the time frame that you can devote to this cause. Reaching that goal may be years away. For health reasons, family reasons, or career reasons you may not be able to remain active on this issue beyond a certain point. That's OK. Citizen campaigns are like relay races. Someone picks up the issue and runs with it as far as he or she can. The baton is passed on to many other runners. While you're running, you give it your best effort. Look around for a good person or group to hand the baton to. Ask them to take it and give it their best effort, aiming straight for the campaign goal. If you're lucky, you may still be around—or able to come back—for the final leg. In any case, you played an important part in making a citizens' campaign happen.

Measuring Campaign Goals

Not every worthy civic campaign is successful, if success is measured in terms of resolving a problem. Campaigns such as Habitat for Humanity and food banks may never solve the problems of poverty. The measure of their success has to be how much they help people. Many other campaigns, such as animal welfare causes, also don't develop an ultimate solution, but they surely contribute to improving the quality of life for many creatures. Civil rights campaigns have yet to create the ultimate American dream of social equality, but each can provide a step toward the mountaintop Martin Luther King Jr. pointed to in his 1963 "I Have a Dream" speech.

Many civic campaigns are like that. An immediate goal may be met, but the ultimate goal is still far off. Yet the small steps are necessary if there is to be any hope of reaching the distant goal. Runners, walkers, wheel-charioteers carrying the torch burn out and pass it to others. "Voluntary organizations have a continuing shift of membership. Like a river they constantly change," observed Owen D. Owens, whose passion has been preserving trout streams from the ravages of pollution, starting with one near his backyard in suburban Pennsylvania. In *Living Waters: How to Save Your Local Stream*, he summed up a philosophy of life developed in grassroots organizing.

"Keeping the purpose in mind to evaluate what you have done helps you learn from successes and failures, and grow stronger," Owens wrote in an astute assessment of the elements of organizing grassroots volunteer groups. "Our goals keep us moving in the right direction, stirring us up when we get complacent and encouraging us when we feel despair. . . . If as a leader you can get people to begin to listen to each other, you will be half way toward accomplishing your goals. . . . Life comes into an old movement as people get inspired and are willing to take the responsibility to do something new."

The newest wrinkle in grassroots organizing is the World Wide Web, which potentially gives quick access to resource information and other activist groups around the world. Some civic groups establish Web sites to promote their causes. These function as electronic newsletters, offering another way of alerting a network of activists to upcoming events. They can be very useful for researching an issue and seeing what others have done to address it across the country or internationally.

One Web site, for instance, offers "The Electronic Activist," which features numerous how-to guides to various aspects of organizing and running a civic campaign. These guides are reprinted articles from *Freedom Writer*, a newsletter published by the Institute for First Amendment Studies, an organization founded to "counter the political activities of the religious right." A guide called "Tips for Activists," for example, advises, among other things: "Give individuals within your organization room to be different and understand that they are not all there for the same reasons. There might be multiple ways of doing things, and individuals might join your cause for different motivations than your own." That's sound advice for any campaign.

Besides new tools like the Internet, veteran activists also rely on old-fashioned checklists of things to do, people to call, letters to write, meetings to attend. Keep these handy on notepads, clipboards, electronic organizers, whatever you find easiest to use. Review these frequently and check things off. Then you can tell at a glance what's been done and what needs to be done. To help establish this organizational frame of mind, there's a checklist for engaging in civic activism at the end of this chapter. Alert organizers periodically check themselves out to see if they are still on course, or whether it's time to ask someone else to provide leadership in a certain direction or handle a crucial campaign task.

"Keep your eye on the prize," says Jeff Tittel, executive director of the New Jersey Sierra Club, who worked for a decade as a volunteer in a grassroots environmental group, Skylands CLEAN, that was credited with halting various large-scale development plans for forest tracts in the mountains ringing the Wanaque Reservoir water-supply system by mobilizing local citizens and networking with the Sterling Forest Coalition across the border in New York and the Highlands Coalition on the New Jersey side. "Look at your goal, and everything fits under the goal." Tittel now advises environmental protection campaigns around the state.

To stay on track to reach a citizen group's goal, he said, "you have to have a political strategy. You have to have a media strategy. You have to be able to talk to reporters, develop credibility with them, be able to say and show things in a concise way, that are well documented, so you can get your message out to the media. You have to write your own fliers and newsletters, to get your own media out as well. So it's political, it's media, it's fund-raising. You have to have money. A little bit goes a long way. And you have to develop a legal strategy." A political strategy may include gathering petitions for a referendum; seeking the support of the municipal council, county freeholders, or state legislature; or working with candidates for public office challenging entrenched incumbents who rebuff your campaign's approach. A legal strategy may include filing a lawsuit or a Freedom of Information Act request for public documents, defending against a harassment lawsuit, or knowing when and how to take a civil rights complaint to the American Civil Liberties Union or an environmental issue to the Rutgers Environmental Legal Clinic and asking their attorneys to go to court on your group's behalf.

The following chapters provide an in-depth look at ways of conducting a civic campaign, addressing the political arena, and navigating the news media. A chapter on research materials and other resources follows.

How citizen campaigns work is outside the frame of life modeled in the media. There aren't many role models on television or in the movies, or, for that matter, in newspapers. However, there are people, if you ask around, who do know. Ask various organizations for assistance in the area of their expertise or interest. Build a support network that stretches across the spectrum of the community or region your group is operating in. Master the details of the issue and proposed solutions you favor. Your organization should become a reliable authority on the subject for the news media, government officials, and the public. Ask experts in the field for assistance with research, reviewing materials your group produces, and speaking at events your group sponsors. Double-check facts, quotes, and assertions the group makes.

To use a military metaphor, you are walking point on this issue—and people are watching to see if you step on a land mine or find the path that will advance your group toward its goal in one piece. In reality, your steps are creating a passage, if you navigate past political and social trip wires, that opens the way for potential supporters and the public to follow. It takes courage mixed with a sense of caution and a sharp eye for booby traps—which American society is full of, given its competitive nature. Seek out good guides.

Keep in mind that nothing in life is guaranteed. Some civic campaigns succeed, some fail. Many accomplish only part of their goal. But America would be a poorer place without these myriad grassroots efforts to make it a better society. And if your group's effort doesn't succeed, it might plant the seed for one that does.

Checklist for Civic Action

1. Make a firm commitment to participate in a project, with the goal of staying with it to a satisfactory conclusion or to help the campaign reach a crucial milestone, such as a public referendum. Devote what you feel you can best provide in skills, networking contacts, time, and finances.

2. Organize your life to accommodate this commitment. Plan for the long haul—not a Rough Riders charge up San Juan Hill. Unless you intend to devote every waking hour to this campaign, don't quit a paying job, leave your family, or drop other responsibilities. Budget your time to juggle this new project with family, employment, and other commitments. Reduce time spent watching TV or whatever you know is a waste of time when compared to this project.

3. Pace yourself. Pell-mell activism can quickly burn out the best of activists emotionally, physically, spiritually, and financially.

4. Enjoy yourself. Stop and admire the sunset, smell a flower, jot down a poem or a drawing, hum a favorite song, hug a friend or pet, go jogging or canoeing or window-shopping, amid laboring to save the world.

5. Be professional. Do your homework, research the issues, be well prepared for public presentations. Don't hype the issue beyond the known facts. Don't inflate your credentials to speak to the issue. Don't make charges that can't be proven. Refrain from trading insults with opponents. Make the best possible documented case for the cause you embrace. A citizens' campaign lives on its credibility.

6. Be passionate in your commitment. Convey that passion with creative activities and well-chosen words.

Emotions that flare into verbal fireworks or escalate to threats of violence are counterproductive to a campaign seeking to earn public trust.

7. Be prepared for public ridicule, provocative critics, attempts at intimidation. Engaging in civic action, while usually not as dangerous as life in a war zone, still requires enduring and overcoming hostility from often ferocious opponents.

8. Master the elements of conflict resolution, especially mediation and negotiations. Romantic rhetoric of militant activism such as "burn, baby, burn!" and "revolution!" are nonsensical in suburban and rural regions, while dangerously inflammatory in urban neighborhoods and in dealing with government agencies.

9. Be diplomatic. Citizen campaigns are full of prickly, impassioned people. They revolt against orders or ultimatums. Decisions are most likely to be made by consensus, a vote after vigorous debate or, more rarely, by a revered leader.

10. Master the elements of publicity and dealing with the news media. Reporters and editors like colorful activities, quotable sound bites from campaign leaders or articulate and well-informed spokespersons, and fact sheets. Because of pressing deadlines, they abhor disorganized events that don't start at the scheduled time, don't produce advertised celebrities, and don't make a point that can be summarized in a headline or snappy phrase for TV.

7

Conducting

a Citizens'

Campaign

Like finger-snapping, toe-tapping music, a compelling idea in action attracts people to admire the conduct of a cause and cheer it on. A well-organized citizens' campaign is like a well-tuned marching band. The members move enthusiastically to the same up-tempo beat, play a heart-thumping tune in crisp harmony, and they maneuver together as a polished team. Like Main Street marching bands, activist civic campaigns need the equivalent of conductors, drum majors, drummers, buglers, and an ensemble of other players who work together to form a crowd-pleasing concert on the go.

A civic group, like a band, is made up of various individuals who see a need to work in harmony. Who decides how they work together varies from group to group. Some have a single leader, usually the founder or a charismatic successor, who delegates assignments to members and supporters. Some have co-leaders. Some have multiple leadership. In some groups, decisions are made by consensus of an

132

executive committee. Some leaders are elected, some are self-appointed, and some are recruited by group members. Experienced organizers work to develop leadership skills among many members, so the group can survive and thrive even if its founder or founding generation dies, retires, or burns out. Many civic groups rotate leadership, using people who have various skills—some are adept at organizing, some at administering, some at chairing meetings, some at dealing with the news media.

Unlike textbook models of, say, U.S. presidents who personify entire eras—George Washington as "Father of Our Country," Abraham Lincoln as savior of the Union—citizen campaigns by their nature have many parents. "The kind of leadership we read about in the history books can best be described as one-person leadership," Si Kahn noted in his community organizing guidebook, *Organizing: A Guide for Grassroots Leaders*. "A people's organization, on the other hand, needs as many leaders as it can get. . . . One of the most important roles of an individual leader in a people's organization is to produce other leaders. . . . We need different leaders because that is one way we appeal to different kinds of people. . . . We also need to have a broad leadership group because no matter what we do we will lose some leaders. They may become tired of what they are doing. They may burn out."

Virtually every civic campaign starts small. One or two, or a few, people find they have a common concern and decide to do something about it. "It's really one-on-one relationships in organizing. You build a group not because you're this great big shot and everybody should follow you, but because people are concerned about the same issue and want to work with you together to save this piece of property, or whatever the issue is. So, it's really that you build a group one at a time," said Jeff Tittel, who directs the New Jersey

Sierra Club. In 1987, Tittel cofounded with a neighbor in rural Ringwood a grassroots environmental protection group with a name longer than the roster of members. Skylands CLEAN (Citizens for the Land, Environment, and Neighborhoods) grew within a decade from two founders to hundreds of members and supporters determined to keep a scenic Appalachian mountain landscape on the edge of the New York–North Jersey metropolis from being paved over with housing tracts and industrial parks. By 1998, residents and other contributors, including foundations, provided sufficient funds for Skylands CLEAN to open an office and hire a staff to coordinate volunteers working on numerous preservation projects in Ringwood and neighboring Highlands communities.

When Skylands CLEAN was launched, the fledgling group took its conservation campaign to the local shopping center and to community meetings. "You have to reach out to people," said Tittel. "You have to be visible." The tiny, brand-new group set up a table outside the local supermarket with a display of a map of the sprawling mountain town "showing all the proposed developments, showing all of the beautiful places that could be lost," said Tittel. "That's a very good, visible way for people to see you and see what your issues are about."

Given Ringwood's location just west of the suburban sea in Bergen County and near the route of the final segment of Interstate 287, there were plenty of preservation-versus-development issues percolating. To provide electricity for future development in the region, a natural gas–fired power plant was proposed for a wooded site overlooking the Wanaque Reservoir. The reservoir is the sparkling center of scenic Ringwood. It is also the source of clean water for two million North Jersey residents living in downstream communities. Skylands CLEAN's mission, Tittel repeatedly emphasized, was, "It's up to local groups in Ringwood to protect this water" by preserving the forested slopes whose runoff resupplies the water system.

When the environmental group circulated petitions opposing the power plant among patrons at the local shopping center and at community meetings, hundreds of residents signed. "People who live in rural areas don't want to see smokestack industries, and they don't want to see a threat to the water supply," said Tittel. "We tied the power plant issue not only to pollution and ugly smokestacks but also the fact that we would lose our conservation status [with state planners], bringing in hundreds of condominiums and sewers and all these things that people had historically fought. . . . We ended up getting twenty-five hundred signatures on a petition that we gave to the town council, which in a town like Ringwood is almost fifty percent of the registered voters," he said. "So the council got the message and the power plant died."

Now the environmental group was well known in town. It attracted the attention of municipal officials, who named Tittel to the town environmental commission and the planning board. And it attracted the enmity of development supporters and anonymous purveyors of harassment. "Signs started appearing in the community that said, 'Wise Use is coming.' With that, newsletters started showing up being mailed townwide attacking environmentalists for chasing [property tax] ratables out of town, raising your taxes, likening us to Luddites, tree huggers, eco-terrorists," Tittel recalled. "The reason the power plant was proposed in Ringwood was to bring power up to Sterling Forest for a new town right on our border of thirty-five thousand people. Another of our victories at the time was that we successfully lobbied Passaic County to condemn [the New Jersey portion of] Sterling Forest; they bought two thousand acres of land in Ringwood and West Milford and took them right off the table for development. That was another factor in why Wise Use started showing up. While we were being attacked publicly and vilified, there were these mysterious fliers popping up questioning everything from people's sexuality to their parentage and lineage, their political orientation, trying to smear people as being gays or homosexuals and communists."

Now the environmental activists were on the hot seat. It was not pleasant to be the target of somebody else's campaign. "At first, there was a lot of disbelief and shock," said Tittel. "You just don't expect it, because it's a community and people know each other. Then there was sort of anger. We responded. . . . Not in kind, but with facts." Amid a crossfire of fliers, newsletters, and statements issued by the two groups, residents got a look at two different kinds of campaigns with diametrically opposed methods and goals. "One of the things it did for us was . . . we started to be able to raise good sums of money from within the community," said Tittel. The influx of financial contributions enabled the environmental group to mail its conservation-oriented newsletters to every household in Ringwood. "People realized what the stakes were in town," Tittel said of the boom in boosters when the environmentalists came under attack.

With the power plant a dead issue and Sterling Forest the focus of a popular campaign embraced by governors and members of Congress, the conservation-versus-development battle in Ringwood shifted to a developer's proposal to pay for installation of sewerage pipes to undeveloped tracts from a regional wastewater treatment plant. The sewer line would allow townhouses and other cluster development in a rural community served by septic fields and small-scale treatment plants. A majority of the town council seemed sold on the sewer plan. Given the circumstances, the environmental activists didn't think a petition drive would carry much weight. So they organized a referendum campaign.

Under Ringwood's form of municipal government, non-binding referendums could be placed on the ballot by petition of a certain number of registered voters or by the town council. An overflow crowd of residents jammed into a council meeting to demonstrate support for a referendum. Facing an unexpected sea of determined faces, the council voted on the spot to put the question on the November ballot and agreed to abide by the outcome.

Now all the stops came out on the organs pumped by both sides. Developers and Chamber of Commerce supporters, council members and former mayors lambasted the naysayers and urged a yes vote on what was billed as a limited sewer plan to a portion of the town, in order to bring in additional tax revenue. Environmentalists and their supporters argued that providing a pipeline to the regional sewer treatment plant would open the floodgates of sprawl development, which would cost more in additional municipal and school expenses than the new tax ratables would pay for, while changing bucolic Ringwood beyond recognition.

To conduct the citizens' referendum campaign, a new organization, Ringwood Action Coalition, was formed. It was led by a small group of residents who had not been publicly active before. This enabled Skylands CLEAN to maintain its IRS status as a nonprofit educational organization and to continue its focus of providing a land-use lawyer and planner to counter developers' presentations before town boards. Jeff Tittel played an advisory role in the referendum campaign, while spending much of his time doing research for arguments he and others presented in public hearings on the housing development plans that triggered the request for a sewer line.

"We had all these volunteers painting signs, going door

to door," Tittel said of the referendum campaign, which was conducted throughout the summer and fall of 1994. "That took a lot of organization. We had to organize ourselves as if we were a political campaign. We had a field operation, a media operation, and a fund-raising operation. This was done out of people's houses. We raised maybe five or six thousand dollars for the campaign. The other side probably had forty thousand dollars. But every penny we raised went directly into mail and postage and fliers. People volunteered and painted their own signs. So actually we got a lot more out of it than just the little bit we had."

On election day, in a town in which the reigning Republicans seldom lost an election, voters overwhelmingly rejected the sewer line plan by 3,487 nays to 1,000 yeas. A sobered town council upheld its pledge and dropped the proposal. The housing development plan that required a hookup to the regional sewage plant died. The Wise Use fliers and newsletters quietly ceased.

"One of the nice things to discover is that the people in Ringwood really have an appreciation for nature," Skylands CLEAN's other founder, Jon Berry, told a news reporter on the occasion of the grassroots group's tenth anniversary in 1997. "We have a lot of support from people who don't consider themselves environmentalists, but they want to protect their quality of life." Like many other Ringwood residents, Berry commuted to his job in New York City, where he worked as a public school teacher, while enjoying weekends and evenings relaxing amid a mountain forest just an hour by bus away from Manhattan's siren-blaring, teeming streets.

The grassroots campaigns in Ringwood began to be cited as models for environmental groups in other communities. The New Jersey Audubon Society awarded its 1994 Conservationist Award to Jeff Tittel for his work in Skylands

CLEAN. In 1998, the New Jersey Sierra Club hired him to manage statewide conservation campaigns. From part-time volunteer, whose occupation was working for a direct-mail public relations company, Tittel's passion for conservation had grown into a profession.

"One of the things I always tell groups to do is to do social events," says Tittel. "To have a dance or a pasta dinner is important to raise some money, but also to make things social. Because people have to feel like they belong. And that helps get rid of some of those pitfalls of ego and personality. If you build up trust and friendship as part of that process, it helps eliminate some of those traps. . . . When you get involved in a grassroots campaign, it becomes like an extended family. There's a lot of bonding that goes on. There's also animosity and dislikes and petty this and petty that. The main thing is that you can function together as a group."

In the Skylands CLEAN campaigns, he said, "we all had a role. And we tried not to step on each other's toes or push each other out of the way. As part of an organizing campaign, you have to assess your friends, try to find stakeholders or people who share common interests and common ground with you. Sometimes you'd be surprised, whether it's in the business community or other organizations, Scouts, school kids. We had debates on the sewer issue. We went to different groups in town. We had our own town forum, where we invited people in on the sewer issue, with a moderator at a school. We had both sides [make presentations]. There are a lot of people out there who may not be members of your organization, but it makes them feel like they belong to go to a meeting and applaud you. Or they go to a council meeting and applaud you when you speak. You've got to get the public involved. You've got to keep that dynamic and interreaction going. That's a very important part of any kind of grassroots campaign. That's what our life blood is."

Tittel's basic message when he speaks to Sierra Club chapters and other community groups is that grassroots activists need to look around at their neighbors to find people with needed skills, then ask those people to help a campaign in their area of expertise or interest. The harsh reality is that grassroots campaigns seldom can count on sustained aid, or much of any help, from statewide and national organizations. Such organizations are usually so busy looking at the big picture and raising funds to support their offices, staff, publications, lobbying work, and so on that they aren't eager to get entangled in what may be seen, compared with big battles in Trenton and Washington, as some local issue. "You have to find the resources within your own community," Tittel emphasizes. "There's something to be said for that. By living off the land, you're more involved with your neighbors. And they're more likely to donate and volunteer their time."

While volunteers' time and energy, and the social and political support of other citizens, are the basis of grassroots campaigns, virtually every civic campaign needs to do some fund-raising to pay for essentials such as printing and mailings. The trick is to leverage small to modest amounts of money into invaluable accomplishments. Fortunately, this is an arena most Americans know something about. "Raising money is an American tradition," notes author Si Kahn. "Look at all the churches and synagogues that were built by people's own hands with money that they raised together. . . . People are always putting on fund-raising drives to help co-workers who are hospitalized, to establish a park for the neighborhood, to build playground equipment for a local school, to support charitable organizations. Millions and millions of dollars are raised in this country each year."

Kahn's organizing guide listed forty common fund-raising events used by community groups—from dinners and festivals to raffles and rummage sales. In addition, he notes, grants are sometimes available from private foundations and government agencies. These are often awarded on a matching basis, requiring that a similar amount be raised from other sources. Institutions that award grants generally make it clear that they are providing seed money for community groups that are expected to develop local sources of fundraising to sustain them.

"We did bake sales," Jeff Tittel recalls of the way Skylands CLEAN launched its fund-raising efforts. "You get forty people involved baking cakes, which you then sell to another forty people. At the end of the day, you stand there for eight hours and you may only make two hundred dollars, but three or four hundred people have gone through, seen that you're credible, you're part of the community. And that's the important part of doing something as simple as a bake sale." Other basic fund-raising activities include membership dues, walkathons, door-to-door canvassing, and benefit concerts.

Another familiar example is the thermometer poster that many community groups use in dramatizing the progress of a fund drive. Effective fund-raisers create a network of various sources of money, provide continual feedback on progress toward the campaign's fund goal, and keep clearly posted accounts of the fund's income and payment of expenses. "Sometimes a people's organization gets the idea that it's not important to keep the kind of detailed financial records that a business keeps," Si Kahn writes, raising a crucial point. "In fact, it is probably more important for a people's organization to keep good, solid, reliable, and understandable financial records . . . [because] an organization's financial records can be used to discredit or destroy it." Government grants are likely to be closely audited. Nonprofit groups that raise over a certain amount annually from the public and from grants are required to file a financial statement with state government.

One of the benefits of networking with other organizations is that a small community group need only raise sufficient funds to put out mailings and fliers in its community, perhaps send representatives to travel to Trenton or Washington to lobby, and pay for other incidental costs. Free meeting space can often be found at a church, school, library, or nonprofit agency. Visiting speakers or delegations (such as international citizen-diplomacy groups) can be housed with host families. More substantial fund-raising—collecting money to buy a wilderness parcel or urban property for parkland, for example—can be funneled through a larger nonprofit organization with expertise in that area and staff to handle the accounting and other paperwork. In some cases, a municipal or county government is willing to be the lead agency in raising and administering funds for buying property or creating a sister-city program. Carefully research the options of networking with established nonprofit organizations or government agencies if the funding needed for a particular campaign exceeds the abilities of a community civic group to raise and administer.

Conducting a civic campaign is an ongoing learning process. No one has all the answers. Every situation involves a different set of circumstances. What worked one time may not work in the next instance. That's because circumstances are always changing. The people involved in one campaign will surely be a different mixture, or have some changed attitudes, in the next controversy. The most common ingredient in successful grassroots groups is persistence. They don't give up. They don't fade away. When the winds are blowing against them, they sail another tack. When the winds shift more favorably, they're ready to unfurl all sails and make straight for the port of their goal. And in the end, the public may quickly forget there ever was a civic campaign that provided or saved something now taken for granted. But campaign activists can feel a tremendous sense of accomplishment. "It's a warm feeling," said Jeff Tittel, "driving around Ringwood and the Highlands, seeing people walking or swimming on land we saved. People forget: We have places to enjoy because other people fought to save them."

Pitfalls

What can go wrong in a citizens' campaign? Plenty. Cofounders can have a falling out, or a power struggle, over who's really in charge or what direction to take when things don't go well. Abrasive leaders can repel members, potential supporters, and the news media. The campaign actions of some members—burning the American flag, for instance—can give the organization a tinge of radicalism that members of the public, let alone potentially sympathetic government officials, don't want to be associated with. Some campaign activists may be secretly working to sabotage the cause.

"One of the things you have to wonder about, or at least I do, is what are people's motivations when someone joins a group," says Jeff Tittel. "Do they want to take over and push everyone else aside? Are they really concerned about the issue? Or are they really a plant from the other side? In CLEAN, people became members because they participated. To try to weed out people who might be plants, we had them volunteer to do things, especially something visible. A person who works for the developer or the other side I don't think is going to want to stand in front of the supermarket handing out fliers. It visualizes them to the community as being part of your group. They'd feel very uncomfortable. You also never send out somebody who's new without someone who's experienced. It's part of the training—people don't always know how to volunteer and hand out fliers or whatever. On the key strategies, very few people were in the loop." That is, not everyone active in Skylands CLEAN's campaigns was invited to strategy meetings. These were conducted by a core group who knew each other well.

Another tactic to take, which I favored when active in Vietnam veterans' and citizen diplomacy campaigns, is that strategy, tactics, and everything else should be discussed in meetings open to the public. Any secret meeting of some members could be construed by some government agency as a conspiracy for planning illegal activities. Eight relatively new members of a Vietnam veterans' organization I had been a founder of were indicted by a zealous federal prosecutor on charges of planning to attack the 1972 Republican convention in Miami with various weapons, including slingshots and fried marbles. When the case came to court a year later, the main witnesses were government informers who had been the people at a small meeting of veterans in Florida who suggested switching from peaceful protest to violent tactics. The actual protests at the convention were peaceful, in the tradition of the organization. The jury found the indicted veterans not guilty. But in the meantime, government officials who didn't like the fact that there was a Vietnam veterans' organization working for peace in Vietnam trumpeted it in the press and to Congress that it was a hotbed of violence and sedition.

In working to create a citizen-exchange project with people in the Soviet Union, organizers were under close surveillance. FBI agents would sometimes show up at an organizer's workplace or church or home and announce that they wanted to talk with so-and-so. When that happened, the person meant to be put on the hot seat politely talked with the G-men, telling them exactly what we planned to do—travel to the Soviet Union, invite some Soviet citizens to visit America, and work together to reduce tensions to help prevent nuclear war.

We also had to contend with anticommunist groups furious about making any contacts with communists. My approach, which other organizers agree with, was to invite the FBI, anticommunist groups, and anyone else who wanted to come to attend our planning meetings. These were usually held in a church, which provided neutral ground where visitors, of course, were expected to be on their best behavior. These meetings were also held in various towns throughout New Jersey. So anyone with ill intent had to do a lot of work to keep up with our planning and organizing of a wide-open, constantly growing citizens' campaign.

When the leadership of a civic group falls out, two things usually happen. Either the group splits into two vigorously competing groups—or it tears itself apart into feuding factions. Competition is the elixir of American life. For that reason alone, lots of civic campaigns split, like amoebas, into two vigorously growing organizations. Should that start to happen, there's no sense trying to stop a human impulse that can be as powerful as any other natural force. Look at it like this: now the issue you felt was so crucial has two hardworking champions. Cooperate with each other when and where you can. Swallow the bitterness of parting close company. Make it an amicable divorce.

When a breakup is bitter, many civic activists drop out. When the Vietnam veterans' group I cofounded began to splinter into warring political factions, each convinced it was more ideologically correct than the other, I hung up my boonie hat and jungle jacket and decided it was time to become a plain old unadorned, unattached citizen. I had been a reluctant activist to begin with. I wanted to be a writer. I felt more comfortable writing poetry laying bare the emotional land mines of war and working as a journalist investigating issues from a skeptical, but nonpartisan stance. I did not want to be an activist ever again—until nuclear war clouds darkened the horizon in the 1980s.

Some people are content to be an activist once in their life and chalk up the outcome, victory or defeat, to experience. The generation of Americans who came of age in the 1960s is full of such folks. They may look back at their civil rights/antiwar/women's lib experiences fondly. Or they may look back bitterly. In the 1980s and 1990s, many of those old activists heard another call. They got involved in the nuclear freeze/citizen diplomacy/Central America/Middle East/recycling/conservation/urban revival/AIDS/Agent Orange campaigns. They brought not only previous experience, but maturity. They were acutely aware of the pitfalls of civic campaigns waged idealistically. They brought, I felt, a refreshing breeze of seasoned common sense into the public arena. They worked to apply lessons learned from past experience to newer or different issues.

Then there are people who are virtually lifelong activists. As soon as one campaign ends, they're organizing another one. Often, they juggle several causes at the same time, as well as a job and family life. These people are gold mines of savvy experience. They know how to pace themselves and stay active on issue after issue without burning out. They sidestep pitfalls seemingly instinctively. They are well worth seeking out for advice, not to mention inspiration.

The ultimate pitfall is success—or, rather, apparent success. "We won a major battle in Ringwood and then the town turned around and changed their zoning to allow one-acre [development] on the mountains," said Jeff Tittel. "We won a major victory with Sterling Forest, but still what's left could jeopardize what's won. Sometimes you win the war and you lose the peace. That's why you always have to be vigilant and keep fighting. One piece of property in Ringwood, citizens have stopped development on it four times. The guy's coming in again. When you're active in grassroots issues, it's always vigilance. At Great Swamp, they won this great victory. They kept out the airport. But they never did a watershed management plan." Now the wildlife refuge designated as wilderness by act of Congress is ringed by housing developments and corporate campuses. Addressing the latest conservation victory ballyhooed by two governors, Tittel said, "Does Sterling Forest become like Central Park, surrounded by development, or does it become [part of] a contiguous greenbelt in the Highlands?"

Some civic campaigns—maybe every one—take more than one generation of activists to protect what was won.

8

Addressing

the Political

Arena

Civic action is not civil war. This is not
Robert E. Lee and his West Point–trained brethren squaring
off to determine on bloody battlefields whether the United
States should split into two—slaveholding versus nonslave-
holding—republics or remain one nation. Civic action is a
very different sort of patriotic campaign. Its strength is a
creative mix of nonviolent confrontation and bipartisan
cooperation on issues generally fought out in the political
arena. It is a less heralded side of American culture, in which
we are raised from birth to take sides—in sports, politics,
religion, region, race, gender, global affairs. We are not used
to cooperating with other people, especially not with those
viewed as opponents. Indeed, American culture is so competitive that we have a hard time cooperating with family
members.

A crucial element of effective civic campaigns is establishing bipartisan and nonpartisan credentials. "Bipartisan"

is a term usually associated with Democrats and Republicans supporting the same piece of legislation, such as a Green Acres bond referendum. At the community level, the concept applies to political partisans of all sorts. Keep in mind that most voters are neither registered Democrats nor Republicans. The biggest bloc of voters in New Jersey is undeclared. That's a category that covers a wide range of political attitudes, from apathy to anarchism, socialism to hard-right conservatism. Many other voters register as Independents. Acknowledging that big mass of unaffiliated voters, some communities hold nonpartisan elections for municipal government. "Nonpartisan" means that candidates run for mayor and council or school board seats as individuals or on informal slates rather than on political party tickets.

For civic campaigns, raising the banners of bipartisanship and nonpartisanship puts Democrats, Republicans, and partisans of other political passions on notice that this campaign is not aimed to favor any party but instead welcomes members of competing parties and political beliefs to support a cause for the common good. For the campaign to succeed, this stance has to be absolutely genuine, not slick political rhetoric. Organizers and volunteers have to make it very clear, in word and deed, that when working on behalf of this campaign there is no hidden agenda to provide some group with a political advantage. That takes enormous self-discipline for people accustomed to taking sides politically. There may be lapses. People may have to be reminded what bipartisan and nonpartisan mean. Focusing all of those competitive energies toward achieving the same goal is one of the keys to a citizen campaign's success. For the politically astute, which most politicians are or aspire to be, that is also its appeal. They have an opportunity to be associated with a popular cause.

Another crucial element of a civic campaign is ecumenicalism. That means welcoming the participation of Buddhists, Catholics, Jews, Muslims, Protestants in all their theological variety, and members of nonmainstream religious groups that often get labeled as sects. Americans are more divided by religious beliefs than by political persuasion. Yet one of the most impressive developments of the late twentieth century was the grassroots spread of various religious groups working together on social issues in an ecumenical spirit. This has meant churches, synagogues, and Islamic centers opening their doors to help host community-improvement campaigns, provide forums on various social problems, and provide assistance to disaster victims locally, nationally, and globally. Keep this in mind when doing outreach. Meet with a variety of religious leaders. Some prefer to support soup kitchens, others peace campaigns. They may be offended *not* to be asked, when a survey of religious groups in the community is done. Send a polite appeal letter to each congregation. Include each on your mailing list when sending out notices of upcoming events. Ask that the event be listed in the religious group's bulletins. Many groups are happy to be asked to help a community campaign.

The same applies to business groups, labor unions, veterans' organizations. Don't assume that Chamber of Commerce members are only interested in promoting their business, or that unions only care about their members' welfare, or that veterans only care about rehashing old war stories. These three groups, plus social organizations such as the Elks and women's clubs, provide much of the volunteer spirit in American communities. Other founts of support for civic activism in many communities are YMCAs, YWCAs, Jewish community centers, public libraries, public and private schools, and colleges. These institutions often post announcements of community events on their bulletin boards, host community events, and help with myriad organizing details for numerous projects.

And then there's municipal government. This is the level of government at which citizens can attend a public meeting and speak directly to elected officials. Many civic campaigns have been launched in a municipal council chamber and sustained by ongoing debate and dialog at successive public meetings. This is an arena that generally gets regular newspaper coverage. It is an arena where issues and proposed solutions can get a thorough airing, especially if a case can be made that the community is going to be affected and there is something municipal government can do about it.

Dealing with municipal officials takes persistence and astute diplomacy. At many council meetings, speakers from the audience are limited to three minutes or five minutes. Rather than demand more time, read from a prepared statement. If time runs out, hand the statement to a supporter to continue reading from. State your case as briefly as possible. Unless your cause is the First Amendment, staging a battle over how long you can speak will bury whatever other case you wanted to make. It won't get heard amid the shouting about who sets the rules. Use some creativity to get your point across. If you are blocked from making your statement, then of course raise the issue of denial of free speech.

Local officials may dismiss your cause as outside their bailiwick. It's up to your campaign supporters to convince them otherwise. This is where a community network comes in. If local officials get lots of letters, faxes, phone calls, and statements from people in the community, they'll take the matter seriously. Unless it's a completely local issue, civic campaigns generally ask for a resolution of support from the mayor and council to take to the state legislature or

Congress. Lining up support and getting that resolution is good experience for lobbying state and federal officials.

Before heading to Trenton or Washington, start with meetings with staff aides in representatives' district offices. Raise the issue and your campaign's proposed solution with these aides. Ask for the legislator's support. If there is a bill that would provide funding or other assistance to further your campaign's goal, ask the legislator to sign on as a co-sponsor. This is a good way of tracking how bipartisan support for this bill is building. Provide materials to help the aide brief the legislator. If something needs to be voted on in the near future, ask for a meeting with the legislator. Mobilize your network to write, call, and otherwise get in touch with legislators. Make use of your supporters' political and social affiliations with legislators—Republicans contact Republicans, Democrats contact Democrats. Keep an eye on developments in the legislature or Congress; prepare someone from your campaign to testify at committee hearings. Ask a legislative aide for advice on length of the testimony and details of making the delivery. Take extra copies of that written testimony to the hearing to provide to news reporters.

A little-known facet of government and politics is that busy legislators often rely on knowledgeable citizen groups to research an issue, develop proposed solutions, and even draft proposed legislation. This is why networking with legislative aides is a very important first step. These are the people who can teach you the legislative ropes. Many civic movements, religious groups, unions, and veterans' organizations have offices at the state and federal level for lobbying. These offices are another source of advice and assistance. So may be staff members in state agencies or the governor's office, if you gain an ally there. Other helpful sources may be municipal and county officials who know their way around Trenton and Washington.

An often overlooked level of government is county government. In New Jersey each county legislature is called, for peculiar historic reasons, the board of chosen freeholders. Its elected members often got their start as municipal officials. They generally have some political clout with state government. If asked, they often willingly consider voting a resolution of support for a civic campaign that either affects their county or is based in their county.

On some issues, as I discovered in working to prevent nuclear war, county officials are eager to send a message to Washington—or Moscow. This is a level of government that is generally as approachable as municipal government, filled with people who may live in your community or a neighboring community, who see their bailiwick as helping residents of the county in numerous ways. The Democrats and Republicans on the Essex County Board of Chosen Freeholders considerately listened to my proposal to create a county peace office aimed at helping prevent nuclear war. When I found some potential funding from a private foundation, they voted unanimously to put my project under the county umbrella. They sent resolutions in support of reducing Soviet-American tensions through diplomacy to Washington and, hand-carried by me, to Moscow. They greeted the first Soviet delegation to arrive in New Jersey as part of the citizen-exchange program that the Essex County Office on Peace helped to create.

Some activists dismiss working with government as selling out, being co-opted politically, or engaging in a meaningless gesture of working with officials who have no respect for grassroots participatory democracy. All of these dire things can happen, if civic activists bend under the weight of politics-as-usual. On the other hand, a well-organized and focused citizens' campaign can bring out the best in government officials. And sometimes, the smallest symbol of government-citizen cooperation can carry great weight that advances a grassroots cause.

To promote the work of the Essex County Office on Peace, I had business cards printed in red, white, and blue and handed them out liberally in New Jersey and on my travels in the Soviet Union. When a Soviet citizen-exchange delegation arrived at Kennedy International Airport in the wake of a spy crisis, suspicious U.S. customs officers questioned the group's claim that these citizens of the Union of Soviet Socialist Republics had been invited to New Jersey by some peace groups. A telegram they produced from US-USSR Bridges for Peace in Vermont only provoked more questions. Did the Soviets have an official host in New Jersey? Who was responsible for them? The head of the delegation produced one of my Essex County Office on Peace cards. "Here is an official host," he later related in telling this story. The Russians were waved through customs.

Effective civic activists know how to address a wide variety of audiences, from friends and neighbors to religious congregations to government officials. They seek to convert skeptics into supporters. They forthrightly engage opponents in public debate whenever possible in whatever forums are available—municipal council meetings, state legislature hearings, community forums. When they speak, they cite facts. They summarize the opposing camp's arguments and describe how that outcome would affect this audience. They contrast that with how their campaign's proposed solution would affect people. They keep it clear that the object of a citizens' campaign is to win converts, not demolish opponents. Even in a rip-roaring public debate, they make it clear in their demeanor and choice of words that their campaign aims for dialog, that it seeks people working together to create the best solution for the issue at hand.

Pitfalls

Politics is the graveyard of many good ideas and reform movements. If an issue is closely identified with one candidate or one party seeking elected office and that person or party loses the election, an idea they championed often goes down to defeat as well. That is why bipartisan and nonpartisan campaigns usually have better success: they are not tied to who wins or loses an election; instead, their aim is to demonstrate so much public support that the campaign goal gets accepted by whoever holds elected office.

Political battles can create bitter enemies. Demonizing opponents in a civic campaign is counterproductive. Citizen groups that engage in emotional battles with other people scare off volunteers, use up valuable time and energy, and may find themselves suckered into a debilitating fight that derails the focus of the campaign. Sometimes the worst battles can be with a competing civic group.

Make it clear that you are building a bipartisan or nonpartisan, ecumenical, broad scale campaign for the public good. The most effective response to a combative opponent is a smile and a handshake. The best retort to a verbal threat is to quote Abraham Lincoln: "The best way to destroy an enemy is to make him a friend." Or Pogo, the cartoon backwoods philosopher: "We have met the enemy and they is us." The best response to a physical threat is to call the police and the news media. Make it clear that you are not going to be intimidated, that you expect the issue to be dealt with fairly on its merits, and you expect to be treated the same way.

Making demands of government, without clear-cut public support, can backfire. In *The Activist's Handbook*, Randy Shaw, an urban housing organizer, presents a telling example of how not to win friends and influence people. Some militant activists shifted the focus of a campaign on behalf of homeless people in San Francisco from the need for more affordable apartments to the "right" of squatters to live in a city park. Setting up camp and panhandling in the park raised the hackles of city officials and other park users. "Once homeless advocacy became identified with defending unpopular individual behavior rather than working to ensure housing . . . public support for progressive approaches to homelessness declined," he noted. "The strategic and tactical errors made by homeless activists flowed from their willingness, even eagerness, to fight a battle on their more powerful opponents' terms. Some social change activists seem to seek out these David-and-Goliath struggles, apparently believing that defeat will be tinged with nobility."

There are two warning lessons in this example. First, a campaign can be shifted from its original goal by a small group of militants bent on raising another issue, unless campaign organizers forthrightly state in public that a breakaway group is pursuing a different issue but the original campaign has not altered its goal. Too often, Shaw notes, civic activists hesitate to air internal disagreements while the thrust of their campaign is being diverted to other aims. Second, civic campaigns need not only to raise an issue but also to present a workable solution that attracts solid public support. "A good program will put policymakers (instead of advocates) on the defensive," Shaw wrote, "by forcing them to respond to the agenda set forth by the social change organization."

Political activity can get rough. There can be fierce infighting over the direction and goals of a campaign. There can be harassing catcalls and phone calls, and nasty letters from ominous, anonymous sources. Some activist tactics, such as blocking streets and marching on the White House, may be perceived as threats by people in power and treated as such. Some tactics, such as civil disobedience, invite physical response—even abuse—by police and probing of an activist's private life by prosecutors.

Unless you plan to get arrested in an act of civil disobedience, a civic activist's wisest course is to be a model citizen. If you plan to do civil disobedience, prepare for jail and time in court. If you have young children, plan who's going to take care of them while you're in court or behind bars. If you have no intention of spending time in jail, you also have to be well prepared—to avoid it. Activists have been targeted by zealous prosecutors, the IRS, and the FBI. Expect to be closely scrutinized by the powers-that-be. Activists I worked with were arrested on charges ranging from possession of marijuana to allegations of planning to assault the 1972 Republican convention in Miami (a federal charge lodged against a group of antiwar Vietnam veterans that ended in a jury acquittal more than a year later). Be careful what you say and do. Be wary of anyone who urges you to do something that is illegal. Somebody could be trying to set you up to be arrested—and sidetracked from the civic campaign.

The best way to counter politically motivated prosecutors is to conduct your campaign and your life in a completely aboveboard manner. Unless your cause is legalizing marijuana, stay away from the stuff. Unless your cause is refusal to pay taxes for one reason or another, pay your tax bills. If you're campaigning for safer streets, don't go racking up speeding tickets rushing to lobby in Trenton. On the other hand, if you used to be a speed demon but have since seen the light, tell people that this is where you are coming from. Speak about the issue from your experience. It is another way to demonstrate that people can change their attitudes and actions.

Politics, at bottom, is about power of one sort or another—power derived from might, money, or popularity. Despite the romantic image of Thoreau, Gandhi, or Martin Luther King Jr. sitting alone in jail and by their moral witness speaking truth to power, what grassroots activists most need in order to prevail are allies, lots of allies. And if those allies include a wide cross-section of the community, the powers-that-be take due notice. And if those allies include some members of the powers-that-be, the forces of intimidation think twice or more. And if supporters of the campaign grow to a certain critical mass, the forces of intimidation dissipate.

You never know who might be an ally until you ask people to support your campaign. You may have to ask more than once. You may have to work hard to convince people that you know what you're talking about and have a workable solution to the issue you've engaged. It's possible that your initial efforts won't succeed. The timing may be wrong. People may not accept your proposed solution or believe that your campaign can pull it off. The campaign may need to take a creative turn and come up with another approach. Conservation groups, for instance, often start off calling for government action, then find they make better progress by organizing a fund-raising drive to buy an endangered scenic spot. When the buyout campaign has lined up an impressive amount of public support, government officials often develop an interest and contribute to the fund-raising drive, providing just enough to take it over the top—and, not incidentally, taking credit for saving a now-popular corner of nature.

"The question of whether or not to become involved in

electoral politics is one that is difficult for many organizations to resolve," Si Kahn notes in his guide to community organizing. He lists the problems: political campaigns are all-or-nothing, win-or-lose situations; sympathetic candidates who win may not honor their commitments to the cause; and supporters of the grassroots cause may split over the choice of candidates.

On the other hand, Kahn argues, there can be merit in a citizens' campaign running its own candidates for public office, especially at the local level. Candidates for elected office get taken more seriously by the news media and the public. At the school board and municipal council level, an energetic and articulate civic activist has a reasonably good chance of winning a seat. From that seat, he or she can gain more visibility for the civic campaign's cause. "An electoral strategy that comes out of the experience of an organization's members, that focuses on issues, that is centered around not just elections but a continuing strategy to influence government," Kahn writes, "can make a real difference in all our lives."

Any number of civic campaigns in New Jersey demonstrate that this is the case. Electoral and other forms of politics can be very useful tools for citizen activists, if handled with care.

9

Navigating

the News

Media

There are two things soldiers fear more than machineguns—giving a speech and dealing with the news media. (I exaggerate, but not much.) Citizen activists usually have the same fears, which stem from people being petrified they might look foolish. Nonetheless, two of the most effective tactics that civic campaigns employ are presenting memorable public speeches and making compelling subject matter for the news media. Journalists are often attracted to cover a speaker on a controversial topic and then are impressed by a dramatic delivery. Giving a news interview is like giving a speech. The more succinct it is, the more likely that pithy segments will be quoted.

Fear of speaking in public is a widespread phobia that requires more than courage to overcome; it requires practice. Famous actors still get butterflies in the stomach before each performance. But they've learned the value of preparation. Once onstage, they give a performance that was much rehearsed and reflects the time spent rehearsing. Civic activists need to do the same. Write down what you want to say to other people about your campaign. Read it out loud—to yourself. Get used to the sound of your own voice, and you won't be so startled in public. Read the draft of your speech to a friend, family member, fellow activist. Discuss whether anything should be clarified, added, or deleted. Study how other people give speeches. Army sergeants and many other speakers begin lectures on serious topics with an unexpected joke. It breaks the tension, and it engages the audience, which feels an instant sense of camaraderie.

Giving a toast to hosts in Volgograd, a Soviet city full of grim reminders of World War II battles, I directed my remarks to a fierce-looking, medal-bedecked veteran who stood barely five feet tall: "Come visit America," I said, echoed by our translator, "so Americans can see for themselves that Russian soldiers are not all 10 feet tall." An explosion of laughter among Russians and Americans instantly bridged the Cold War divide. If trying to be humorous makes you uncomfortable, simply start with a statement as to who you are and why you are involved in this campaign. "Hi, I'm Eve Adams. And I'm worried that my grandchildren won't be able to experience nature's wonders that I enjoyed when I was growing up, if we don't do something to save the garden in the Garden State." Ask your audience to consider certain facts and the likely outcome if people don't do something to change the situation. Present the campaign's goal. Invite questions and comments. And have a dialog with those who respond. Before you know it, you'll have forgotten your fear of talking in public—although you may soon worry about how to stop! Ask people to sign a petition, take some literature, make a financial donation, write or call a government representative, volunteer to work in the campaign. Thank them for listening to you. Provide telephone numbers, addresses, Web sites where they can get more information.

Many speakers use visual aids—slides, videotape, poster-board displays. These help attract the audience's attention and present the campaign's case. Using visual aids requires some preparation. Avoid the embarrassment I once brought on myself, when I appeared in a high school classroom with a borrowed slide projector I'd never used and proceeded to give a demonstration in fumbling with an infernal machine that insisted on running the slides in backward sequence. (I was saved by an alert student who knew what to do.) If you are technically challenged, ask someone more capable to handle the visual aids.

Once you've given a speech combined with visual aids you're ready for television. Actually, in a TV interview or talk show, all the technical stuff is handled by other people. You just sit or stand where they want you to be and talk when they give you cues. What you need to concentrate on is conveying your message briefly, clearly, and memorably. Have a few well-considered sentences in mind to tell what the campaign is about and what people can do about the issue. Stick to what you want to say, despite whatever the interviewer may say to you. If asked to comment on some other controversy, return the focus to your campaign. Say something such as: "I haven't formed an opinion on that— I'm here to talk about what we can do about this issue." Or: "Speaking of that, here's how it's related to our issue." Watch how other people handle TV and radio interviews. Who impressed you? Those who cited facts, expressed personal opinions, or conveyed both? If looking into the camera makes you nervous, look only at the interviewer. Talk to him or her in the same way you engage anyone else you talk to on this topic.

Being on television may be the least of your worries.

How often is that likely to happen? A far more common fear is likely to be: How do I write a press release? Many civic groups delegate publicity to a volunteer, who often doesn't have a clue what to do. It is easier, I assure you, than appearing on television. What news editors want in a press release is a brief outline of *who* is doing *what* (you're giving a speech on a burning topic), *where* (place, street address, town), *when* it is happening (date, time), *why* (what's the issue?), and telephone numbers for one or more contact persons who can provide further information. News editors want to know this information as far in advance as possible. Depending on the news value of the issue, editors may favorably react to a faxed notice the day of an event. But it had better be a hot topic. Otherwise, they prefer several days' notice, so they can decide whether to cover it as they look over everything else the newsroom may be covering that day or that week.

What do news editors look for when leafing through a pile of press releases? It depends on the type of newspaper—community, regional, national—the event, and the source. Top priority goes to press releases about state and federal court decisions, arrests for major crimes, activities by the governor and other prominent officials. News editors also look for advance notices of civic campaigns and community activities in their paper's coverage area. "Newsworthy items may include projects for civic and environmental improvement, information about people making a difference or up-coming events," states a brochure on "How to Prepare a Press Release" prepared for civic groups by editors of the *Record* and North Jersey Newspapers, which cover much of North Jersey via two daily newspapers and numerous weeklies.

A basic strategy for getting newspaper coverage for an event is first to mail or fax a brief, one-paragraph notice long in advance (call and find out the deadline, which could be four to six weeks before the date of the event) for use in community bulletin board sections. Call a couple of days later, ask to speak to the person in charge of that section, and ask if your event notice arrived. If not, send another. Ask the person you speak with when you should send a more detailed press release and to whose attention. In the longer (one to two pages) press release include the basic data about the event, plus quotes on the topic by one or more organizers, giving a reason readers should care about the issue. After sending that release, make a follow-up phone call and ask if it arrived. Ask if the newspaper will run an advance story, as well as cover the event. One reason for doing this is to alert readers who might want to attend the event.

Ask to speak with an editor or reporter who covers that town or specialized beat, such as environmental coverage. Most editors and reporters, in my experience, are happy to talk with representatives of civic groups. They may hedge on whether the event itself will be covered, because that's a decision that is finalized that day. If an airplane crashes or any number of other things pop up, the reporter may well be sent elsewhere. If you get coverage of the event, great. If you don't—but got a community bulletin board notice, an advance article, and a discussion or meeting with an editor or reporter—you have made your group known for future coverage possibilities, such as feature stories. And you know how to do a press release for the next event.

Make a contact list of all the newspapers circulated in your community. Buy one of each at a newsstand or take a look at them in the library. Editorial page mastheads, and sometimes a box on page two, convey addresses and phone and fax numbers. Many papers now also have Internet addresses. Weekly and daily newspapers have different deadlines, even different personalities. Talk with an editor or reporter at each paper and find out to whom you should address press releases for news coverage and bulletin board notices. In the New York metropolitan area, the *New York Times, Daily News,* and *Post* cover things of interest to them in the suburbs and rural fringes. Radio, television, and many newspapers rely on the Associated Press for information on upcoming events. If your event has regional interest, send a press release to the Associated Press (in New Jersey, there are regional offices in Newark and Trenton). Ask that your event be listed on the "day book" for that date. If it's deemed newsworthy or unusual enough, the AP may even have one of its reporters cover it. Then you may hear a summary of your event on news radio or get a clipping of the Associated Press account that appeared in a distant newspaper, or even your hometown paper.

At weekly newspapers, which have small staffs, a well-written press release may go directly into the paper with minimal editing. Now you are deciding what readers will see. So make it interesting and to the point. Look at how newspaper articles are written, with a lead sentence designed to catch a reader's eye, followed by informative details in easy-to-skim short paragraphs. Double-check that your press release includes the date, time, and place of the event. List who is putting on the event and name community sponsors or supporters. Briefly convey the purpose of the event. Provide at the top of the release a contact person or persons, with day and evening telephone numbers, for journalists to call for confirmation or additional information. If there is reason to provide a phone number for the public to call for more information or to order tickets to a fund-raiser, include that number and area code in the press release.

Sometimes, a community newspaper doesn't have staff available to cover an event. In that case, ask if you can submit a second, follow-up press release about what happened at the event. This may require building some trust with an editor to demonstrate that you can be relied on to give an accurate account of what occurred. And remember that it must be submitted quickly to meet that newspaper's printing deadline. The follow-up press release can be a simple switching of tenses in the first release—from an event "is to happen" to it "happened"—with the addition of any significant details about the event that were not in the initial release.

On pages 167–168 is a press release that formed the basic text for a news article published three days after a Monday event in a weekly newspaper published on Thursday. A very similar press release was previously sent to news organizations across the region, announcing that the event would be taking place. The initial press release generated news accounts in area daily newspapers and coverage by three television stations and several radio stations. An Associated Press feature story on this atypical suburban event was carried by newspapers across New Jersey and by the Philadelphia *Inquirer*. Given all the television and radio news coverage, daily newspaper articles, and buzz through town, the generally skeptical editor of the weekly *Montclair Times* could feel confident that the event indeed occurred and the follow-up release hand-delivered to his office was an accurate account.

This is a basic press release format. Double-spaced, it fits on two pages, with room to spare. It conveys the essential details of a civic action. Not every press release can rely on such dramatic elements; widespread news media interest in this particular community event in January 1984 was whetted, of course, by international events. To heighten interest in what jaded journalists often see as humdrum community events, media-savvy civic activists point up

For Immediate Release

Contact: Jan Barry (201) 123–4567

"NUCLEAR WAR AND MONTCLAIR" BOOKLET
MAILED TO EVERY HOUSEHOLD IN TOWN

A copy of an information booklet on what citizens can do to help prevent nuclear war was mailed Monday to every home and business in Montclair. Some 15,500 copies of the booklet were delivered to the Montclair Post Office in a post-Christmas pile of 45 mail sacks which were accepted by Postmaster William Frye.

The Montclair Nuclear War Education Committee, which prepared and distributed the booklet, titled "Nuclear War and Montclair: Is There a Place to Hide?," noted that the booklet is just the first step by the local residents in a campaign to enlist the grassroots power of ordinary Americans in the international effort to avert a nuclear holocaust. The next step in the campaign is to work toward the establishment of a sister-city relationship with a community in the Soviet Union.

"As Jesse Jackson's successful journey to Syria to obtain the release of Navy flier Lieutenant Goodman has demonstrated, sometimes the appeal of concerned citizens can reach across borders which governments have turned into armed camps," the committee noted in a prepared statement. "We believe that concerned citizens of the United States and Soviet Union can work together to help release us all from the threat of nuclear war."

Houston, Seattle and Jacksonville, Fla., presently have sister-city relationships with the Soviet cities of Baku, Tashkent and Murmansk, the committee noted.

Support for the local booklet on nuclear war prevention has come from a wide variety of community leaders and organizations, including U.S. Senator Frank Lautenberg of Montclair, members of the Township Council, local leaders of both the Democratic and Republican parties, members of the clergy and such groups as Congregations for Peace, Educators for Social Responsibility, Physicians for Social Responsibility and the YWCA.

At a fund-raising event held Sunday at Union Congregational Church, which was attended by 150 people, a number of artists, including opera singer George Shirley, gave performances to help defray the costs of printing and mailing the booklets.

their activities' connections to larger events—unless the campaign is focused on a local issue. Whatever the case, press releases that catch news editors' attention convey an interesting idea or speaker or event and contain some specific details of what a citizens' campaign is doing to address an important issue, citing examples of what others are doing elsewhere or a summary of where the action idea came from. They clearly state the goal the group is aiming to achieve. And they invite the public's participation. Newspapers are in the business of conveying interesting ideas and events that they hope will catch readers' attention.

As this example illustrates, press releases can be written or rewritten right after an event, describing what happened, and submitted to newspapers that have time to get the report into the next edition. An initial press release announcing what is going to take place, where, and when should precede the event by several days. Indeed, a civic campaign seeking wide news coverage should be producing a series of press releases, each tailored for the requirements and interest of various news organizations.

Writing an attention-getting press release is one of the last steps in putting together a worthy civic action that garners news coverage. For journalists, there has to be more than sizzle—there has to be something interesting cooking. What became a highly newsworthy event of mailing nuclear-war-prevention booklets to every home and business in a town took much of a year to develop. It began when several people got together to talk about what could be done to educate their neighbors on this issue. A committee was formed that did some research into the idea of a booklet, which had been done in some communities in other states. A core group of about six people then attended town council meetings, seeking official support and funding for such a public education booklet. They pointed out that the federal government required the municipal government to maintain a plan for the evacuation of Montclair in the event of nuclear war. The citizens' group argued that, given the deadly range of nuclear warheads and speed of missiles, this was a fatally flawed plan for a densely populated state. They suggested that a better idea was to educate the community about how people could help prevent nuclear war. A full-fledged debate about the role local government should play in addressing the danger of nuclear war raged for several months in the town council chambers. The group wrote and rewrote a draft booklet that was reviewed and publicly debated by municipal officials. When the council majority declined to provide funds for the booklet project, the committee and a growing network of supporters reached out to community groups to raise three thousand dollars to cover printing and mailing costs.

It was time consuming, but raising the issue with the municipal government generated a stream of news articles, letters to the editor, and editorials in the weekly newspaper. When the town council declined to provide taxpayer funds to print an information booklet, most of the money needed for the project was raised in a single fund-raising event, which drew 150 people during a snowstorm, including council members who contributed as individuals. The drumbeat of local coverage built up interest among the regional news media, which reported the story as a major event when the citizens' group produced its booklet and took mailbags full of copies to the post office.

Press releases are a vital ingredient in public education for a civic project. They are essential tools in an effective press campaign. With sophisticated planning, a civic group or coalition of groups can produce a coordinated series of news releases statewide (or regionally) and in several communities at the same time.

On pages 172–173 is a statewide news release, which
included an attachment providing a daily schedule of where
members of a Soviet peace delegation would be in various
New Jersey communities over the course of two weeks and
a list of local contacts with phone numbers. Besides this
statewide release (which also went to New York and Philadelphia news organizations), others were sent to local newspapers announcing where members of the Soviet delegation
would attend public events and visit schools and colleges
on certain days at certain times in area communities. This
took a lot of effort over the course of months to line up
hosting groups in a number of towns and cities, schedule
various events, and produce a coordinated barrage of press
releases. The result was an outpouring of press coverage from
one end of New Jersey to the other day after day for two
weeks. In newsroom after newsroom, reporters competed
to see who could write the most interesting story on Soviet
visitors interacting with hometown New Jerseyans.

This news release was timed to correspond with the
arrival of the Soviet delegation in New Jersey. Because of
the abysmal Cold War communications between the Soviet
Union and United States, it wasn't certain when Soviet visitors would arrive until they showed up at Kennedy International Airport from Moscow. Once this group's arrival was
confirmed by a telephone call, this press release was quickly
faxed to news organizations. Local press releases were also
issued by local hosting groups. When daily newspaper articles appeared the next day, editors at weeklies who got
similar press releases could feel assured that real live Russians were coming to town on schedule, and alert their readers about it when their paper came out a few days later.

Besides press releases, newspapers also welcome neatly
written letters to the editor and opinion essays. Look at how
other people write these. Do they make their point in 250

For Immediate Release

Contact:

Jan Barry (201) 123–4567

Patricia Compton (609) 765–4321

SOVIETS ARRIVE
FOR US-USSR BRIDGES FOR PEACE
CONFERENCE IN LAWRENCEVILLE MAY 13

PRINCETON (May 8)—15 Soviet visitors from the Russian region of Volgograd arrived today for a two-week stay in the United States, during which they will live with American families and participate in a citizens' peace conference on Saturday, May 13, in Lawrenceville.

The conference, entitled "Building Bridges for Peace: A US-USSR Dialogue," will be held at the Lawrenceville Presbyterian Church from 1 p.m. to 6 p.m. Before and after the conference, the Soviets will be guests of families in communities throughout the state and will participate in a number of community forums, visit schools and colleges, churches and businesses.

The Soviets' visit and the conference are being sponsored by New Jersey–Volgograd Bridges for Peace, a coalition of church, civic, and educational groups which includes the Coalition for Nuclear Disarmament in Princeton, Episcopal Diocese in Trenton, The Hudson School in Hoboken, Pax Christi of Monmouth County, Presbytery of New Brunswick, Ramapo College, and South Jersey Bridges for Peace.

The Soviet delegation—which includes teachers, journalists, economists, a Russian Orthodox priest, a surgeon, an artist, engineers, and factory workers—has traveled here to inaugurate a joint project linking New Jersey with Volgograd (formerly called Stalingrad) in an ongoing series of citizen exchanges.

"New Jersey is one of the first states to be linked with a region of the Soviet Union to continue the vital process of creating peaceful relations between our nations," says Jan Barry, of Montclair, a writer and Vietnam veteran, who is one of the exchange coordinators.

Barry and Patricia Compton, of Pennington, president of the Delaware-Raritan Girl Scout Council and a representative of the Episcopal Diocese of New Jersey, visited the USSR in 1986 with a Garden State peace delegation sponsored by US-USSR Bridges for Peace, a citizen exchange organization based in Norwich, Vermont. In 1987, a Soviet delegation made a reciprocal visit to New Jersey, laying the groundwork for discussions that led to linking N.J. and Volgograd.

Barry and Compton will lead a 20-member Garden State delegation to Volgograd in September, as the second part of the 1989 citizen exchange.

"We look forward to meeting with our Soviet counterparts at the conference in Lawrenceville and discussing how we can work together to address not only preventing nuclear war but also other problems facing us all today," says Compton.

words or less (the typical length of a published letter to editor)? An opinion essay may run twice that length. Some papers allow 750 words. Whatever the space allowed, it is another chance to make a case for your group's cause. In many towns, people avidly read the letters to the editor of the local newspaper. So you might get stinging replies, or supportive ones, in future issues. Rotate letter writers, so the same person isn't always on the firing line. Refrain from firing off a letter to the editor on everything that riles you. Editors appreciate people who soberly weigh in occasionally with something meaty to say, as opposed to people who simply seem to be opinionated about everything. Check facts that you cite in a letter to the editor as carefully as those stated in any document put out by your campaign. Address the issue and proposed solutions, rather than what you think of an obnoxious opponent. The object of a letter to the editor (really a letter to other newspaper readers) is reasoned persuasion, not scoring debating points.

A trade secret of the news media in America is that its major sources include the public—ordinary citizens who call, write, fax, e-mail, or personally deliver an interesting tip or complaint. That's the genesis of many news accounts, from spectacular fires to defective-product recalls. While government officials and political candidates are masters at garnering news media coverage, spinning out their versions of the world in press conferences and press releases, they don't have a monopoly on the media. Besides tips on newsworthy events unrelated to politics, journalists also look for "man in the street" input on headline issues, new social trends sweeping or creeping through society, and "whistle-blower" revelations of crime and corruption in government. They also engage the attention of the masses with tales of murder, mayhem, and misfortune committed by, against, and among ordinary people. Citizen activists provide another level of input into journalism, input that can set the tone of coverage of a community or an issue.

Consider that unless someone objects to something at a school board or municipal council meeting, there is no controversy. With no questioning, no give and take, no raised voices, such meetings are routine sessions of government. Routine official meetings are boring to journalists and are treated as such. But add a spark of controversy and now there's something interesting to report. That's a basic fact of journalism. It is also a basic fact of democracy. Until some citizen raises some issue, the citizenry is playing no role in the conduct of public affairs at the community level of government. Many journalists in America not so long ago used to mock citizens who rose to speak with any regularity at municipal meetings as "gadflies," gabby kooks with nothing important to impart. Now, perhaps because it's no longer politically correct to call anybody disparaging names, citizens who rise to speak more than once at public meetings are more likely to be treated as activists, a name that implies upholding an honored American tradition of dissent and democratic discourse.

Yet that contempt for kooky gadflies still lingers in newsrooms. "Are these people credible?" an editor sometimes grills a reporter on citizens who challenge local officials. That notion that these are kooks is often reinforced by incensed officials who call editors to object to news coverage of some upstart's challenge to authority. This can be a make-or-break stage for a new citizen campaign. Civic activists must make their case to a tough, skeptical audience of news editors. If they do, news coverage in that community may well shift to focus on the merits of the controversy that was raised from the grassroots. If campaign spokespeople come off as not credible, the issue and its advocates may well be buried in a news media whiteout that relegates the whole thing to the status of an unmentionable nonissue.

Citizen activists often act as though, since they know that they are right, the world *has* to listen. It can be a rude shock to discover that, while you're absolutely convinced of the facts and burning importance of a certain issue, the rest of the world is on a different wavelength. Experienced activists provide fact sheets on an issue that journalists, officials, and other interested parties can double-check for themselves. They stick to the known facts and a reasoned interpretation of these facts to state their case. Unless they have proof, they don't accuse public officials of crimes. If they intend to make such a case, they better have evidence to show journalists and other investigators, including prosecutors, or they lose credibility.

Typically, citizen campaigns are aimed at getting government to do something or stop doing something. In that case, government officials are potential allies to be won over to the merits of the campaign issue. Sometimes, campaigns are raised in municipal council meetings to generate press attention to an issue that local government can do little or nothing about—foreign policy, for example. The fact that "what can we do about the threat of nuclear war?" is discussed at a municipal council meeting is news. During a debate on that subject at a Montclair Town Council meeting, a majority of officials were skeptical of engaging residents on this issue—until one councilwoman pithily stated that this was the closest level of government to citizens, one at which people could speak with public officials face to face and raise their concerns. That has been the case in community after community regarding environmental pollution and many other national or global issues.

But when a mere citizen raises the issue of nuclear war,

Agent Orange, or peace in the Middle East at a municipal meeting, not only skeptical officials but news editors want to know that the grassroots advocate has done some homework and knows what he or she is talking about—and has a thoughtful proposal about what people can do about the issue. The news angle is that an important national or international issue is being discussed at the community level. The level of this discourse is set by those who initiated it. This is one way that community activists make news and develop credibility with journalists, officials, and the public.

Developing credibility with journalists is a must for gaining ongoing coverage. To this end, every encounter with a news reporter is important. Do you ramble and stray off the point? The reporter, looking at his or her notes, has nothing to quote that relates to what you have to say about the issue you set out to address. The reporter may write a summary of what he or she thought you meant to say. It may well not convey what you are trying to say and do. Providing a handout of your group's position on the issue helps a reporter see what your campaign is about. He or she likely will ask you questions to clarify your stand and why you decided to get involved. Tell the reporter a brief summary about yourself. Don't play coy about what you do for a living. If you are unemployed, say so. If you are a housewife, janitor, part-time worker at a fast-food restaurant, say so. If you are a business executive, police officer, or journalist, say so. If there is good reason not to identify your employer, say that.

Journalists want to know who they are talking to, where they are coming from, and what the ground rules are in talking about a person's life. If one of your concerns is possible pressure on your job because of speaking out, tell the reporter that. Most journalists respect that concern. But they like having an activist's work and home telephone numbers to call when seeking comments. If there is a reason you never want to be called at work, state that and decline to provide your work number. See if a fellow activist is willing to be called at work when comment from the campaign is needed by reporters during the day. Or provide a pager number, with assurance that you or someone else will call back as promptly as possible. The last impression you want to leave with journalists is that you are some sort of mysterious, shadowy character. They will either set out to do an expose of you and your campaign or shy away from covering you altogether.

This does not mean community activists have to reveal their private, personal lives. It does mean showing reporters that you're a responsible citizen. One way activists do that is by doing more research on an issue than anybody else around, and sharing that information with reporters and the public. It means providing reliable, factual, timely information and the sources of that information, not simply repeating your opinions. It means making brief persuasive arguments aimed at busy fellow citizens, not haranguing reporters and audiences at length. It means being polite to rude reporters and patiently answering dumb questions from people who seem totally ignorant of the issue. Educating journalists, who generally are juggling several diverse assignments, is hard work. It is among the most important work that civic activists do. Take the time to make sure reporters understand what your campaign is about. Ask to meet with editors and explain your case to them as well. These are the people who edit the reporters' copy and decide how it is displayed. They should size your campaign up for themselves. Your presentation to editors should be brief, to the point, and professional. Know something about the person you're talking to. If you happened to attend the same high school or college, or your children attend the same elementary school, it may help break the ice to say so. But don't presume to tell a news editor how to do his or her job. They tend to get offended. Ask editors to include your campaign and its issue in the paper's coverage. Present them with a well-organized press kit (a folder with a fact sheet and background information on your group, at a minimum) and a leaflet and press release on any upcoming event. Such a meeting usually makes the most sense when you are seeking coverage of an upcoming event. It also makes sense if your or your campaign has suddenly become the center of a controversy.

If some journalists seem set on doing a muckraking exposé of your campaign, you have two choices. Refuse to talk to them. Or tell them you welcome the exposure but expect it to be factual and fair-minded. It is not usually so clear what reporters are up to when they ask probing questions. Journalists tend to be abrasive even when they are simply trying to understand the scope of their assignment. They usually have to absorb a lot in a hurry: they've got deadlines to meet, editors breathing down their necks to get this assignment done fast and get on to the next one. In addition, people being interviewed often ramble and don't get to the point. That's why questions are likely to fly. Give short answers, rather than the long version. Be candid about the origins of the campaign, the (probably small) size of your membership, your lack of organizing experience. Grassroots groups are composed of ordinary citizens, not professional political campaign organizers or polished politicians. If a reporter forgets that and questions stray far afield from the issue your campaign is addressing, say so. You don't have to answer questions about your sex life or anything else unrelated to being a civic activist.

"When I read quotes from activists that seem curious or ill-conceived, invariably I am told that the remarks emerged in the course of a long, on-the-record discussion that veered from the original focus of the reporter's inquiry," notes Randy Shaw. "There is no law requiring activists to talk at length to reporters or to provide comments on diverse issues on which they are unprepared to speak." By his account, Shaw's experiences with California journalists have often been adversarial. Dealing with the New York news media can be like that—"in your face" reporting, ambush interviews. That hard-nosed tabloid style of reporting also goes on in New Jersey. Learn when to call time out, by saying, "This is off the record, right?" Get a confirmation that it is off the record, or stop the discussion. Many reporters like to hear and recycle gossip about people and political campaigns. Be wary that some caustic comment you make about someone else isn't going to end up in a news report. Unless you know the reporter well enough to be assured that off-the-record comments stay out of bounds, stick to on-the-record statements.

Journalists are likely to be sympathetic to civic campaigns. They see much of the dark side of American life, and the lack of solutions from government agencies. "Reporters enjoy interviewing real people with real problems, because so many of their interviews are with skilled spin-control experts," notes Randy Shaw. "The natural demeanor of community speakers, combined with reporters' sympathy toward them, generally produces a positive story." It's been my experience as a civic activist and as a news reporter that most journalists like doing reports on citizen groups tackling a serious issue. But there are always exceptions.

If a news report, feature story, or an editorial on your campaign is a hatchet job or just plain awful, you and campaign supporters can write letters to the editor in rebuttal. One or more might get published. It demonstrates to editors and readers that your campaign isn't folding under pressure and isn't going to allow itself to be misrepresented. If a glaring factual error is made—the name of the campaign was misstated, a quote was attributed to someone who didn't say that—call or fax immediately and ask for a correction. Provide the correct information, such as the actual statement made by the misquoted person. If the slant of the news piece or editorial is unfavorable to your campaign, that's an opinion, which you naturally find fault with. But it's not an issue of facts. Getting a "correction" to a difference of opinion will take convincing adversarial journalists to take another look at the issue and your campaign.

One way to prod hostile journalists to rethink their stance is to continue doing outreach to other journalists, who may very well have no ax to grind. Or do have an ax to grind regarding their competitors. "Responding to unfair [media] stories is . . . difficult," notes Shaw. A letter of complaint to the editor/producer/reporter may generate a followup report giving your campaign's side of the issue. "An even better tactic is to contact a competing media source and give it the opportunity to cover the story correctly," Shaw writes. "Media organizations enjoy the opportunity to demonstrate that their competitor missed critical facts." Whatever course you take, don't let a nasty encounter with one news organization sour your campaign's relations with the rest of the news media.

Study the news media to determine what and whom to contact. Weekly newspapers generally provide coverage of anything interesting taking place in the community or communities they cover. This can mean anything from running a bulletin board notice of a potluck supper at a local church that is hosting a guest speaker from your campaign to putting a feature story about your group with photos on the front page. A daily newspaper that covers a wider region is generally more selective. Its editors may ignore your press releases until they decide it's time to weigh in with their region-oriented take on your campaign. You may need to cultivate reporters and editors at a daily newspaper for a while before gaining coverage. In doing this outreach, also include columnists who might take an interest in the issue. Send letters to the editor focused on aspects of the issue and your proposed solution. Inquire about writing an op-ed essay on the topic. Newspaper staffs are constantly seeking fresh ideas to grace every page, from the front page to the travel section. If your campaign involves travel overseas, contact travel editors as well as news editors.

Besides newspapers, check out magazines that might have an interest in covering the issue your campaign is addressing. The most likely to be interested are regional magazines and specialty magazines. Some may assign a staff writer, a freelance writer, or commission someone with your group to write about the issue in depth. In doing this outreach, send copies of press coverage your campaign has received. Don't overlook newsletters of supportive organizations. Consider putting out a newsletter for your campaign. This can provide supporters with campaign updates between news coverage and spread information about the widening scope of that coverage.

For civic activists who persevere, time spent cultivating news media coverage can be well worth the effort. News articles and radio and television reports validate citizen campaigns to supporters as well as potential allies. They confirm for other journalists, government officials, and the public that this campaign is worthy of serious attention when it comes to this issue. Many times, I have tracked the progress of public education on an issue by watching the increasingly more sophisticated coverage in newspapers and on television and radio. News coverage in the United States is a two-way street. Civic groups that have something important to say and tackle tough issues can get as much attention in the press as celebrities, without having to hire a press agent.

Keep in mind that news organizations don't cover what they don't know about. Your campaign events are not going to be advertised by your opponents. Crucial facts you feel are important to evaluating the issue may not be known by reporters or the public. These facts may remain unknown if your campaign doesn't bring them to the attention of the news media and the public via forums, newsletters, and other forms of outreach.

If you want journalists to call your campaign for comments on breaking news in your civic group's area of interest, you've got to provide them in advance with names and phone numbers of articulate campaign leaders. Journalists keep lists of possible sources for quick comments in various categories, such as environmental matters. When a policy pronouncement comes out of Washington or Trenton, a hazardous spill occurs along a highway or river, a chemical factory explodes, reporters flip quickly through their phone lists to see who they can call for comment. "The quality of reporting influences public perception, and from public perception, often, comes public policy," note the editors of *The Reporter's Environmental Handbook*. Among the recommended sources of reliable information listed in this handbook for journalists covering environmental issues are government agencies, industry associations, academic experts, and a few civic organizations. If reporters haven't heard from credible citizen ecology groups that provided contact names and phone numbers, their sole sources for environmental news reports will be government officials, industry spokespersons, and academic specialists. The same is true for other issues.

Pitfalls

"The news media never gets it right," is a common complaint. From misspelled names to mangled quotes, there is certainly plenty of evidence of errors in news reports. Dealing with the news media can be maddening. Years ago, I spoke at an event in New York that was covered by a network television station. On the eleven o'clock news show, there was my name on the screen—identifying another speaker. I called the station and asked for a correction. At the end of the news program, a correction was broadcast: the name of the speaker misidentified as me was provided correctly under his image—and my name flashed on screen with a video clip of yet a third person.

There's not much that anybody else can do about boneheaded goofs by journalists. But civic activists can help keep them to a minimum. Harried reporters filing a story on deadline can make unintended errors when they try to decipher hurriedly jotted notes. In the absence of a press release, fact sheet, copy of a speech, or hearing testimony provided by a civic campaign, they have only their notes and memory to rely on. If questioned on some point by an editor, the reporter has no document to counter an editor's interpretation of what was said or done. Editors, by the nature of their job, make snap decisions on what goes into a news report, based on their understanding of the situation, which is based upon what they read and hear at some remove from the actual events. So the more concisely focused information a civic campaign provides, the better.

The key word is "concise." Don't overwhelm journalists with reams of material. Once, an antiabortion activist called the newsroom where I worked to complain that her group did not get as much space in a news story about a federal court decision as the other side had gotten in quoted comments on the case. Invited to provide some information about her group, the activist promptly delivered a large cardboard box full of books, magazine articles, and stacks of other materials. It was too much to contemplate in a busy newsroom. The box was set aside, its contents unexamined. A press kit folder with a few select items would have been scanned and filed for future reference. Some people, when interviewed, talk the same way as the lady with the large box. They ramble on and on, with any quotable comments lost amid a torrent of words, as time runs out for the anxious reporter to get something usable and file the story before an impending deadline—which the wound-up speaker is utterly oblivious to. Needless to say, journalists shy away from repeating such experiences.

Beyond media errors and bias, the responsibility for what kind of news coverage a civic campaign generates rests on the civic group. Run a pig for president, as Yippies did in Chicago in 1968, and that is how the group will be portrayed forevermore in the media. Wave guns in the air, as Black Panthers did in California in the 1960s, and that is the enduring media image of the group. Have families protest and relentlessly testify at government hearings about toxic waste buried in backyards in their community in Love Canal, New York, and that is the enduring media image of that civic action campaign. Choose both a media message and delivery that fit your goal, because once a media image is formed, that's your group in the eyes of the public. Be careful what you wish for in news media coverage.

In covering community meetings, I've been astounded more than once to see an angry knot of citizens arrive and stare right past the two or three newspaper reporters sitting there taking notes and loudly declare that nobody will listen to them. "We're gonna call the news media!" someone will shout out. "We'll get Channel 2 [4] [7] [9] in here!" Newspaper reporters who cover local community events can only shake their heads in wonder at such clueless behavior. The news media that cover that community on a regular basis are there in the room. Television reporters may or may not come to town to broadcast this group of residents' complaint. If they do, it quite likely will be as a result of reading a compelling account in a local or regional newspaper. That's the genesis of many TV news reports.

Should TV camera crews come to town, they most likely will do one or two reports and move on to other things. The excitement of the community issue being on TV will soon fade. The newspaper reporters covering that community will still be covering that community. If concerned residents continue to ignore that reality, they will continue to be frustrated by the level of news media coverage. In the end, it's their call. Civic campaigns usually get the quality of news coverage they work for.

10

Research and

Resources

Action without research is perhaps the deadliest pitfall in civic activism. People who attack a social problem, government program, or some development or plan they object to without a command of relevant facts, including precedents and other viable alternatives, generally get zapped by the powers-that-be. Research and development (R & D) is an integral part of corporate America and many government agencies. On a more modest but no less crucial scale, it should be a key component of any citizens' campaign that wants to be effective.

Research can range from deep slogging through community and college libraries, surfing the Internet, scanning newspapers and magazines, getting on the mailing lists of compatible organizations, ordering relevant government documents, taking a college or adult school course that focuses on some aspect of the issue, interviewing veteran activists, to asking your mother. (My mother almost invariably has an uncannily apropos story about someone she knows who wrestled with exactly the same problem.) Doing research for a civic campaign is an ongoing process, not a cram session for a final exam. It is a continual seeking out of useful information, potential networking contacts, inspiring ideas, and creative tactics and strategies to be considered. That information is shared with other campaign members, thoroughly discussed, digested, and, when it fits, developed into an integral part of the project.

Library research is aided immeasurably these days by the wealth of information available via the Internet. Public libraries and college libraries have established Internet search networks that can presumably locate virtually anything. Library staff may help you focus your search through this electronic maze. If you have a computer at home or at work that is connected to the Internet, you can do a lot of research at your own pace.

Insert some key words—such as "grassroots," "organizing," "activism"—in an Internet search program (such as Yahoo) and depending upon the search engine you will be directed to links with a variety of resources, from magazine and newspaper articles to the Web addresses of activist organizations. Sorting through it all to find material useful to you, however, can be time-consuming. Not every site is reliable—check out who's providing the information on a given site. One Web site I found boasted that it had created computer links to more than three thousand pages of how-to materials. A shortcut in doing Internet research is to follow paths set up by others. Rutgers University's Citizenship and Service Education (CASE) program, for instance, has created links on its Web site to numerous directories established by activist networks. These include the Internet Nonprofit Center (www.nonprofits.org) in Seattle, Washington, which provides an extensive "Nonprofit FAQ" (frequently asked questions) section that provides a menu of links to further information on civic action from "start up" to "volunteer recruitment." The Institute for Global Communications (www.igc.org) in San Francisco offers "Peace-net," "Econet," "Womensnet," and other activist links.

To cut through the clutter, focus Internet research on one thing at a time. Want to know how to create a newsletter using a computer? Numerous Web sites show how to do this, depending on the type of computer and software you intend to use. A Web site called NetAction (www.netaction. org) provides on-line training courses on using the Internet for grassroots activism.

In New Jersey, many environmental groups are listed in an activists' network called Garden State EnviroNet (www. gsenet.org), linked Web sites for community conservation groups, state groups, and national groups. These links provide a variety of research materials on ecology issues, from newspaper clippings to government reports. The New Jersey Sierra Club's Web site (www.enviroweb.org/njsierra), for example, offers an extensive listing of how-to tips provided by its own and other environmental groups' organizers. These range from "Fifteen Tips for Writing a Grassroots Message" to "Get from 'Wish List' to 'Done List.'" The latter tip sheet offers this sort of insight: "Planners ask: Where are we, where are we going, how will we get there? Non-planners ask: Where are we, how did we get here, whose fault is it?"

New Jersey Common Cause and the national office of Common Cause in Washington, D.C., offer organizing and lobbying tips via their Web sites. The national office provides a "Citizen Action Guide," composed of brief passages on organizing civic coalitions and communicating with elected officials and the news media. Besides an Internet site, New Jersey Common Cause, headquartered in Metuchen, offers citizen-training sessions, held in various parts of the state. These provide training for a "Citizen's Army" project it launched that it designed to promote "model clean government ordinances" in municipalities and counter the influence of political financial contributions by special interests.

To aid civic groups and individuals who want to raise an issue with government officials, the League of Women Voters of New Jersey offers an on-line "New Jersey Citizen's Guide to Government," located at www.lwvnj.org. It provides time-tested advice on how best to contact municipal officials, county officials, state legislators, the governor, members of Congress, or the president by mail and telephone. It provides addresses and phone numbers for numerous current officials. "Effective letters are those which are individually written or typed rather than a form letter you simply sign" is the League of Women Voters' topmost letter writing tip. "The most effective time to write about legislation is while it is still in committee" is another astute tip.

Other useful sources of information about government officials and agencies are books such as *The New Jersey Municipal Data Book* and the annual *Manual of the Legislature of New Jersey*. The former provides a statistical profile of the state's 566 municipalities. The latter provides a wealth of information about county government as well as state government, including public information officers for various agencies and a list of daily and weekly newspapers in the state, with addresses and phone numbers. There are similar federal government manuals, including *The United States Government Manual*. Journalists use these and similar guidebooks to find out quickly which agencies handle what and whom to contact to get information on diverse matters.

And, at long last, there is a small but growing assortment of books on grassroots civic activism. I've quoted from a couple that were well researched and, just as important, accessible in bookstores or via Internet booksellers such as Amazon and Barnes and Noble. You may find, after doing extensive research, there is no helpful book addressing the issue you've focused on. Maybe, when you've tackled it with a creative citizens' campaign, you'll write that book.

Selected Resources

Books

Garr, Robin. *Reinvesting in America: The Grassroots Movements That Are Feeding the Hungry, Housing the Homeless, and Putting Americans Back to Work.* Reading, Mass.: Addison-Wesley, 1995. "A Pulitzer Prize–winning journalist visits every state in America to examine hundreds of innovative and successful grassroots programs aimed at helping the poor find jobs and permanent housing and explains the guiding principles behind them."—Amazon.com synopsis.

Hedemann, Ed, ed. *War Resisters League Organizer's Manual.* New York: War Resisters League, 1981. Covers the gamut of civic action, from organizing a community event to marching on Washington and committing civil disobedience at the Pentagon. "Gimmicks to make information or events more attractive may be counter-productive. Very often the gimmick itself becomes the news, not the information which should be treated as news" is a typical hard-won insight.

Kahn, Si. *How People Get Power.* Washington, D.C.: National Association of Social Workers, 1994. "Organizing is a technique, not a mystique. For all the romance about organizing, it is a discipline like any other," Kahn writes from his experience as a civil rights, union, and community activist. This 146-page primer on community organizing is aimed toward developing "poor people's organizations" in places such as rural Appalachia and desolate urban areas where residents are presumed to be powerless and not to have any of the access to society's levers that Kahn assumes the middle class enjoys. His organizing tips provide a good introduction for any citizen activist.

Kahn, Si. *Organizing: A Guide for Grassroots Leaders.* Washington, D.C.: National Association of Social Workers, 1991. This comprehensive 342-page guide to grassroots organizing has been praised by Jesse Jackson, Ralph Nader, Senator Paul Wellstone (D-Minn.), and many other experienced community and national campaign activists. It provides detailed how-to information about organizing strategies and tactics developed from Kahn's work in African American civil rights and multiracial union campaigns in southern states. It is essentially the basic training manual for Grassroots Leadership, a social-change training group based in Charlotte, North Carolina, that Kahn founded in 1980.

Kretzmann, John P., and John L. McKnight. *Building Communities from the Inside Out: A Path toward Finding and Mobilizing a Community's Assets.* Chicago: ACTA Publications, 1997. The authors summarize lessons from community-building projects in neighborhoods across the United States. "The book offers practical advice, helpful tools, and powerful stories that help us see communities in a new way—as treasure troves of talent," states a reader's summary posted on the Amazon.com Web site. The book is used as a training manual by the Community Foundation of New Jersey's Neighborhood Leadership Initiative.

Lakey, Berit M., George Lakey, Rod Napier, and Janice Robinson. *Grassroots and Nonprofit Leadership: A Guide for Organizations in Changing Times.* Gabriola Island, B.C.: New Society Publishers, 1995. "This book is about using teamwork to build and maintain effective organizations," state the authors, who write based on their experiences as multiracial organizers in various social-change campaigns. A typical tip: "How to sustain an organization? You do it by giving people meaningful work, being purposeful, celebrating together, acknowledging good work, and creating a sense of community. If you provide these things people will come and they will stay."

Owens, Owen D. *Living Waters: How to Save Your Local Stream.* New Brunswick, N.J.: Rutgers University Press, 1993. "If somebody wants to do something, give them a way to sign up" is one of many pithy observations by a grassroots organizer of a Trout Unlimited campaign to reclaim a stream that runs through Valley Forge National Park and suburban outskirts of Philadelphia.

Salzman, Jason. *Making the News: A Guide for Nonprofits and Activists*. Boulder, Colo.: Westview Press, 1998. "Landing on *Oprah* is not a strategy," counsels Salzman, a former Greenpeace activist. "Efforts to land in the news should be connected to a larger strategy about how to gain a political victory or make some substantive progress."

Stoesz, Edgar, and Chester Raber. *Doing Good Better! How to Be an Effective Board Member of a Nonprofit Organization.* Intercourse, Pa.: Good Books, 1994. A step-by-step guide by the chairman of the board of Habitat for Humanity International and a management consultant to improving the decision-making process of civic groups large enough to require a board of directors.

White, Barbara J., and Edward J. Madara, eds. *The Self-Help Sourcebook*. 6th ed. Denville, N.J.: American Self-Help Clearinghouse, 1998. A practical, hands-on manual on forming self-help groups, holding effective meetings, doing media outreach and research on issues, problems, and possible solutions.

Internet

"Citizen Action Guide." Common Cause (www.commoncause. org).

"Community Toolbox." AHEC/Community Partners (http:// ctb.1sl.ukans.edu/ctb/).

"The Electronic Activist—Activism How-To." Institute for First Amendment Studies (www.berkshire.net/~ifas/activist/how-to/ index.html).

Garden State EnviroNet "Action alerts" and links to numerous state, regional, national environmental organizations and government agencies (www.gsenet.org).

"Links to Nonprofit Organizations and Other Resources." Rutgers University Citizenship and Service Education program (www. scils.rutgers.edu/case/people.html).

"New Jersey Citizen's Guide to Government." The on-line handbook of the League of Women Voters of New Jersey provides information on various levels of government and tips on how to call and write officials (www.lwvnj.org).

"Nonprofit FAQ." Frequently asked questions about grassroots organizing are answered by the Internet Nonprofit Center, a project of The Evergreen State Society (www.nonprofit-info.org/npofaq).

Peacenet, Econet, Labornet, Womensnet, Conflictnet. Institute for Global Communications (www.igc.org).

"Public Action: A Guide to Environmental Activism—Activist's Toolkit." APL-UW Multimedia Team and Puget Sound Water Quality Action Team (http://nero.apl.washington.edu/activist/activist. html).

"Resources for Nonprofits." Idealist, a project of Action without Borders (www.idealist.org/tools.html).

"Self-Help Sourcebook Online." American Self-Help Clearinghouse (www.cmhc.com/selfhelp).

"Toolkit for Activists." 20/20 Vision Foundation (www.20/20vision.org/tools.html).

"The Virtual Activist." NetAction/The Tides Center (www.netaction.org).

Grassroots Citizen Groups
Citizen Diplomacy, Peace Issues

Creative Response to Conflict/Fellowship of Reconciliation, P.O. Box 271, Nyack, N.Y. 10960–0271. E-mail: *fellowship@igc.org*; Web: www.nonviolence.org/for/fellowship/.

New Jersey Peace Action, 89 Walnut St., Montclair, N.J. 07042; 973–744–3263.

Training for Change, 4719 Springfield Ave., Philadelphia, Pa. 19143–3514; 215–729–7458. E-mail: *peacelearn@igc.apc.org*; Web: www.nonviolence.org/training/.

War Resisters League, 339 Lafayette St., New York, N.Y. 10012; 212–228–0450. E-mail: *wrl@igc.apc.org*; Web: www. nonviolence. org/wrl.

Environmental Issues

Highlands Coalition, New Jersey Conservation Foundation, Bamboo Brook, 170 Longview Rd., Far Hills, N.J. 07931; 908-234-1225. Web: www.njconservation.org.

New Jersey Sierra Club, 57 Mountain Ave., Princeton, N.J. 08540-2611. Web: www.enviroweb.org/njsierra.

New York–New Jersey Trail Conference, 232 Madison Ave., New York, N.Y. 10016; 212-685-9699. E-mail: *nynjtc@aol.com*; Web: www.nynjtc.org.

Passaic River Coalition, 246 Madisonville Rd., Basking Ridge, N.J. 07920; 908-766-7550.

Mutual Aid Self-Help Groups

American Self-Help Clearinghouse and New Jersey Self-Help Clearinghouse, Saint Clare's Health Services, 25 Pocono Rd., Denville, N.J. 07834-2995; 800-367-6274 or 973-625-3037; Web: www.cmhc.com/selfhelp or www.njshc.org.

Neighborhood Organizing

Habitat for Humanity, P.O. Box 2585, Paterson, N.J. 07509; 973-278-4280. E-mail: *PatersonNJ.HFH@worldnet.att.net*; Web: www.geocities.com/Heartland/Prairie/5458//.

Neighborhood Leadership Initiative, Community Foundation of New Jersey, P.O. Box 317, Morristown, N.J. 07963; 973-267-5533.

New Jersey Common Cause, 450 Main St., Metuchen, N.J. 08840; 732-548-9798. E-mail: *njcc@mail.idt.net*; Web: www.commoncause.org/states/newjersey.

Appendix

A self-published pamphlet is an effective method for grassroots civic groups to convey concerns about an issue, offer proposed solutions, and present ways for people to take concerted action to create a popular resolution.

"Nuclear War and Montclair" can serve as a model. It was mailed to every home and business in Montclair, New Jersey, in January 1984 during a tense time of Cold War crisis. The eight-page booklet, written and published by a committee of six community residents, brought a global issue home via a combination of simple techniques: cover art depicting a mushroom cloud rising from the town's location on a globe, drawn by two local students; a conversational text written in a neighbor-to-neighbor tone that distilled months of research by an ad hoc committee of residents; and thoughtful comments solicited from local and regional government officials. Besides presenting a concise array of facts, arguments, and ideas, the pamphlet provided a directory of peace organizations active in the area, a list of books for further information, and addresses of government officials whom readers were encouraged to contact to express their thoughts about the threat of nuclear war.

The booklet committee included Barbara Hammer, a science book author and local business owner; Nan Kaplan, a school media specialist; Doris Schapira, a computer consultant and League of Women Voters activist; Judy Trenholme, a librarian; Pat Wickham, a health food store manager; and myself. It was mailed at a nonprofit organization rate utilizing the YWCA of Montclair's postage permit.

197

NUCLEAR WAR AND MONTCLAIR
IS THERE A PLACE TO HIDE?

"As Emergency Management Coordinator for Montclair I urge every Montclair resident to educate himself or herself about the effects of a nuclear war on Montclair."
— Bertrand N. Kendall
civil defense director

Why should I read this booklet?
This booklet was written as a response to a civil-defense plan for surviving nuclear war, designed for Montclair by the Federal Emergency Management Agency. It is about the frightening possibility of nuclear war, and what we can do about it.

What is the federal civil-defense plan?
Montclair – and all of Essex County – has been designated by the federal government as a high-risk area in the event of a nuclear war. In a nuclear crisis, most of the citizens of Montclair would be required to evacuate to central Pennsylvania. Residents are expected to abandon their homes and join hundreds of thousands of other New Jersey residents in family cars on Route 80, a single escape route. This route is lined with military targets, such as Picatinny Arsenal. For those without cars, rail transportation is promised. Municipal employees, all teachers, suppliers of food, gasoline and other essentials would remain behind, living in a nearby rural county and commuting to their jobs.

The federal plan states that sufficient time would be available to relocate – but in the case of a surprise attack, there would be less than 30 minutes warning time. Under normal driving conditions, the travel time to central Pennsylvania is about five hours.

How can we escape if there is war?
There is no workable crisis evacuation plan for a town the size of Montclair located in a large metropolitan area. The best hope of escaping a nuclear war is the prevention of an outbreak of war. Over the years, people have been trying to find a means of prevention.

• Some seek prevention through greater military strength, hopeful that an even larger arsenal will frighten Moscow (or Washington, in the Soviet view) from launching a nuclear war.

• Other people have sought prevention through a US-USSR mutual and verifiable freeze on nuclear weapons development and deployment. Seventy-five percent of Montclair's voters approved the nuclear-freeze resolution in the 1982 election.

• Some seek prevention through a variety of arms-control agreements.

• Others have sought peace through unilateral actions by nuclear-armed nations.

• And still others seek to escape nuclear war by trying to ignore the whole frightening issue, trusting their lives to fate.

What are the facts?
The Office of Technology Assessment of the Congress of the United States, with the assistance of the Department of Defense and other government agencies, published a report in 1979 called *The Effects of Nuclear War*. The following description is derived from this report.

1

How powerful is a nuclear bomb? How many exist?

One large-sized (20-megaton) hydrogen bomb possesses an explosive power about three times greater than that of all the bombs (including atomic bombs) dropped by all nations in World War II. There now exist some 50,000 nuclear weapons.

Who has the bomb?

In addition to the U.S. and Russia, Great Britain, France and China possess nuclear weapons. India, Israel and South Africa are believed to have them although their governments have not acknowledged it. Other countries that may have nuclear bombs in the near future include Iraq, Libya, Pakistan, Argentina, Brazil, South Korea and Taiwan. Even terrorist groups may be able to make or steal nuclear bombs.

What would a nuclear war do to Montclair?

Situated in densely populated, industrial North Jersey, 17 miles from New York City, Montclair could not be expected to survive even a limited nuclear war.

Anyone who survived a nuclear attack, and the firestorms afterwards, would inherit a toxic world. There would be persistent danger from radioactive fallout. With accumulating doses of radiation, few people could hope to escape cancer, genetic damage or the slow weakening of radiation disease. In a landscape of unburied dead, in the absence of medical aid, garbage collection and running water, epidemics of influenza, typhus – even cholera and bubonic plague – would proliferate. Disease would be spread by flies and other insects that are relatively resistant to effects of radiation.

A large-scale attack on the United States would poison and scorch cropland and harm livestock. Food would be scarce, even if there were means of transporting it. There would be winter without shelter, electricity, gas or oil. There would be armed and desperate people.

Would there be future generations?

The '79 Congressional report on the effects of nuclear war concluded that certain effects that escape calculation pose as serious a threat as measurable consequences. Among the unanswered questions are: How far would firestorms spread? How much would rates of cancer and mutation increase? Would Earth's protective ozone layer survive?

Yet another question, "What would be the effect of nuclear war on the Earth's climate?" has recently been given an answer: Using atmospheric measurements during duststorms on Mars and volcanic explosions on Earth, a group of American scientists has shown that even a small nuclear war would create sufficient dust and smoke to block out sunlight in the Northern Hemisphere and cause a dark "nuclear winter." Virtually all crops would be killed.

2

The various deadly effects of nuclear war could, in combination, make the entire planet uninhabitable and the human species extinct.

What can a person do to prevent nuclear war?
The authors of this booklet have no mandate to tell the people of Montclair what they are to believe. We do share certain beliefs and wish to state them openly:
 • We value freedom and are glad that we live in a country that honors it. We feel that as citizens of a democracy we are all responsible for actions of government. We think it is important to recognize that the tension between the Soviet Union and this country can – as it recently did – result in the deaths of innocent people.
 • We do not believe that Russia or the U.S. seeks a nuclear war. What we do see as enormously threatening is the competition between the two countries to build more deadly weapons and to develop faster ways of sending them to a target. We are frightened by the increasingly automated systems that respond to a possible surprise attack by launching nuclear missiles. Since such systems cannot be entirely free from error, they increase the likelihood of war.
 • We think that a verifiable freeze on the production and deployment of nuclear weapons by the U.S. and Russia is one of the most effective ways to help prevent a nuclear war from beginning.
The people who have endorsed this booklet think that the facts it provides are accurate and important. They do not necessarily share every one of our beliefs. We urge all of you who read this booklet to engage in your own inquiry as to the nature of nuclear war and how to prevent it. (See resource list at the end of the booklet; consult the town library.) Start discussions with other people. Do not assume that someone else can be smarter than you are about this. We also urge you to take action by writing to newspapers and to elected officials.

What are others doing?
Here are other ways that Americans are working to prevent nuclear war:

In town meetings:
The idea of a US-USSR nuclear weapons freeze, a version of which recently was voted by the House of Representatives, originated in townwide discussions in New England.
A number of communities have voted to reject civil-defense plans designed for them by the federal government. Among these are Sacramento, Ca.; Grand Forks, N. Dak.; Houston, Tex.; Little Rock, Ark.; Greensboro, N.C.; New York City – and most recently, the state of Maryland. In Brookline, Cambridge and Newton, Mass., and in Vermont, San Francisco and Boulder, Colo., citizens

3

and local government officials have put together nuclear-war
education booklets distributed to each household.

By curriculum change:
The introduction of nuclear war and peace issues into school and
college curriculums and adult-education programs is presently
under way. Montclair is one of the communities that is considering
how best to include such information as part of public-school
education.

On the federal level, there are now bills in Congress to create a
U.S. Peace Academy. This nation currently supports four military
academies, five war colleges and an extensive ROTC program on
high-school and college campuses, all designed for teaching the
waging of war. In contrast, neither the federal government nor
New Jersey's public education system presently provides any
center of learning for peaceful conflict resolution.

Through people-to-people exchanges:
The better the people in two nations understand one another, the
less likely it is that their governments will misunderstand each
other. Here are some bridges that have been built over the gulf
between American and Soviet societies.

Traveling delegations. A group of American physicians
recently held a round-table discussion about the consequences of
nuclear war with physicians in Russia. This comprehensive,
uncensored and unedited discussion, seen by more than 100
million Soviet citizens, was rebroadcast on U.S. public television.

During the 1982 Christmas season, Ranchers for Peace, a group
from Montana and neighboring states, paid a good-will visit to
Moscow.

Last April the Kansas chapter of Athletes United for Peace were
hosts, at the Kansas relays, to a group of track and field athletes
from the Soviet Union. At first the Kansas invitation went ignored.
Athletes United persevered, and say that they enjoyed a great
week with the Russian athletes.

Sister-city adoption. Just as Montclair has sister towns in Austria
and England, other American communities – Houston, Seattle and
Jacksonville, Fla. – have ongoing relationships with similarly
situated cities in the Soviet Union. An expansion of this idea is
now under way as the Ground Zero pairing project, out of
Portland, Ore., seeks to link hundreds of American cities to
counterparts in the Soviet Union.

As an example of how national relationships can change,
consider our immediate neighbors, Canada and Mexico. Despite
repeated military conflicts in the past, we now enjoy peaceful
coexistence. In fact, the Canadian and Mexican borders with the
U.S. are the longest demilitarized boundaries in the world.
Perhaps our peaceful "borders" can be extended even farther,
even beyond Western Europe and Japan, two other former
adversaries of the United States.

4

"*The better we understand the horror and total destruction that nuclear war would bring to our nation, our community, our families and our friends, the more we will recognize the need for an end to the nuclear arms race. I share the concern of members of our community who are giving this international issue a local focus. I join them in the hope that greater public awareness will prompt effective steps to back away from nuclear war.***"**

— Senator Frank Lautenberg

"*Montclair residents concerned about the issue of nuclear confrontation betwe⁀⁀ ᵗhe superpowers and how such conflicts would affect Montclair will find this booklet informative and thought-provoking. Whatever one's views about the best means of preventing nuclear war, detailed factual information on this issue is essential and this booklet provides exactly that. I commend the Montclair Nuclear War Education Committee and recommend this booklet to the citizens of Montclair.***"**

— Essex County Executive Peter Shapiro

"*I beliᵉᵛᵉ there can be no winner in a nuclear war. The devastation would severely cripple, if not destroy, life as we know it. I think this booklet attempts to point this fact out for Montclair. Governments at all levels have an obligation to move us away from this possible destruction.***"**

— Deputy Mayor James H. Ramsey

"*This booklet and the movie 'The Day After' do not present the dire consequences of a nuclear war for the citizens of Montclair. It would be more catastrophic; the lucky ones would die instantly. I approve the dissemination of information about the consequences. The more we know, the more we can work towards multilateral agreements.***"**

— Councilman Robert W. Eberhardt

"*Weapons exist which have the potential to destroy our planet, yet governments build more. I believe we must join the people of the world in petitioning all governments to stop this menacing escalation. This booklet, prepared by public-spirited, local citizens – and similar booklets being distributed in other communities throughout the country – can provide an impetus for such petitioning. I thank the authors and urge residents to read it.***"**

— Councilwoman Patricia B. Koechlin

"*Nuclear war is no longer a threat; it is almost a certainty. Therefore if the truth is the light, as some people say, it is necessary for all of us to know what nuclear war means. I encourage everyone in Montclair to read this booklet!***"**

— Councilwoman Dolores B. Reilly

December 1983
MONTCLAIR NUCLEAR WAR EDUCATION COMMITTEE
Box 199, Montclair, New Jersey 07042

Design: Gemini

Bibliography

The *Record* is the *(Bergen) Record* of Hackensack, New Jersey.
The *Star-Ledger* is the *Star-Ledger* of Newark, New Jersey.
All interviews were conducted by the author.

1 Citizens in Action

Allee, Rod, "We Can't Do It All with Volunteers." "County Life" column. *Record*, April 12, 1995.

Boyte, Harry C., Heather Booth, and Steve Max. *Citizen Action and the New American Populism*. Philadelphia: Temple University Press, 1986.

Brewer, Caroline. "M.A.N. on Mission to Serve Mankind; Former Pro Athletes Reach Out." *Record*, June 15, 1997.

Briscoe, David. "Report Shows Growing U.S. Reliance on Nonprofit Groups." Associated Press. *Star-Ledger*, November 8, 1998, 35.

Janofsky, Michael. "Demonstrators Say a Conference on Volunteering Is Inadequate." *New York Times*, April 28, 1997, B11.

Kuralt, Charles. Speech at William Paterson College, November 16, 1990. Cited in Jan Barry, "Kuralt's Road Leads Him to Speak in Wayne." *Record*, November 18, 1990, A40.

Lewis, Paul. "Not Just Governments Make War or Peace." *New York Times*, November 28, 1998, B1.

Madara, Edward J. "Mutual Help Via Your Personal Computer." *The Self-Help Sourcebook*. 4th ed. Denville, N.J.: American Self-Help Clearinghouse, 1992.

Paine, Thomas. *Common Sense and The Crisis*. Garden City, N.Y.: Dolphin Books, 1960.

Peterson, Lisa. "Volunteering Is a Jersey Tradition." *Star-Ledger*, April 27, 1997.

Salamon, Lester M., Helmut K. Anheier, and associates. *The Emerging Sector Revisited: A Summary*. Baltimore: Johns Hopkins University Center for Civil Society Studies, 1998.

Tocqueville, Alexis de. *Democracy in America*. New York: Vintage Books, 1945.

205

Toolen, Tom. "Plastics Protest Defeats Big Mac; W. Milford Pupils Lead Way." *Record*, November 2, 1990.
Walsh, Diane C. "Ironbound: Activists' Turf." *Star-Ledger*, February 2, 1997, 21.
Zonenberg, Stephanie. Interview. Paterson, June 18, 1998.

2 *Rebuilding Urban Neighborhoods, Lot by Lot*

Barry, Jan. "Work in Progress; Teens Volunteer to Spruce Up Clifton Park." *Record*, October 10, 1996, L1.
Chadwick, John. "Graffiti Busters; Civic Group Paints a New Image on Clifton Bridge." *Record*, September 29, 1998, L1.
Fuller, Millard, and Linda Fuller. *The Excitement Is Building: How Habitat for Humanity Is Putting Roofs over Heads and Hope in Hearts*. Dallas, Tex.: Word Publishing, 1990.
Kirchner, Joan. "A Gift Home Is Where the Heartbreak Is; Habitat for Humanity Can Assemble Houses but Not Happy Endings for All Who Move In." Associated Press. *Star-Ledger*, March 2, 1997, 48.
McGrath, Mary. "2 Moms Lead Revival of Clifton Parks." *Record*, August 15, 1996.
Traster-Polak, Tina. "Building Hope, One Home at a Time; Habitat Fills Vacant Lots with Dreams." *Record*, February 20, 1995.

Interviews

Baron, Greg. Clifton, June 6, 1998.
Boron, Mary Pat. Paterson, October 30, 1998.
Dunn, Barbara. Paterson, October 30, 1998.
Kaiser, Dawn. Clifton, June 6, 1998.
Sinacore, Mary. Paterson, November 5, 1998.
Sinacore, Tony. Paterson, November 5, 1998.
Smith, Ed. Paterson, November 5, 1998.
Staton, James. Paterson, November 20, 1998.
Zonenberg, Stephanie. Paterson, June 18, 1998.

3 *Saving a Swamp and Other Landmark Campaigns*

Barry, Jan. "Fall of the Wild: 5,000 Trees to Be Cut in Last Legal Logging at Sterling Forest." *Record*, April 16, 1998, L1.
———. "Final $5M Given for Sterling Forest Buyout." *Record*, December 10, 1997, A3.
———. "For the Birds, Mother Nature Spreads Her Wings at the Great Swamp." *Record*, November 12, 1994, B1–2.
———. "Forever Green: States Close the Deal on Sterling Forest." *Record*, February 12, 1998, L1.
———. "Saving the Farny Highlands: Profile of a Grassroots Campaign." *Environment New Jersey*, Summer 1997, 4–5.

————. "Sterling Buyout: 90% Not Enough, Some Say." *Record*, May 28, 1996, A1.

————. "Students Aid Forest Fund: $1,034 to Help Buy Watershed." *Record*, September 18, 1997.

Brydon, Norman F. *The Passaic River: Past, Present, Future*. New Brunswick, N.J.: Rutgers University Press, 1974.

Cavanaugh, Cam. *Saving the Great Swamp: The People, the Power Brokers and an Urban Wilderness.* Frenchtown, N.J.: Columbia Publishing Co., 1978.

Dale, Frank. *Delaware Diary: Episodes in the Life of a River*. New Brunswick, N.J.: Rutgers University Press, 1996.

Dolan, JoAnn. "Sterling Forest Preservation: A Group Effort." *Trail Walker*, the newsletter of the New York–New Jersey Trail Conference, May/June 1998, 8.

Morris Parks and Land Conservancy. "Profile of a Trail Volunteer." *Outdoor Issues*, September 1996, 2.

Morris Parks and Land Conservancy and New York–New Jersey Trail Conference. *Farny Highlands Trail Network: Hibernia to Newfoundland Trail Map*, 1996.

Roukema, Marge. "Sterling Forest Funding a Model for Environmental Protection." Fifth Congressional District (N.J.) press release, August 19, 1997.

Tedeschi, Bruno. "Wilderness Jewel in Peril." *Record*, February 14, 1999, A1.

Whitman, Christine Todd. Speech at Pyramid Mountain Natural Historical Area, Montville, June 9, 1994. Cited in Jan Barry, "Saving Highland Acres." *Record*, June 10, 1994, A3.

Interviews

Fenske, Helen. Green Village, December 3, 1997.

Filippone, Ella. Basking Ridge, May 14, 1998.

Tittel, Jeff. Princeton, April 9, 1999.

4 *Better Living through Mutual-Help Groups*

Barry, Jan. "Troubling Questions about Dioxin." *New York Times* (New Jersey Weekly), September 11, 1983.

Barry, Jan, and Igor Bobrowsky. "Agent Orange." *Daily Record* (Morristown, N.J.), four-part series, May 11–14, 1980.

Brewer, Caroline. "After the Loss of a Child, Healing Comes in Talking to Others." "Inspirations" column. *Record*, January 25, 1998.

————. "The Tangle of the Tongue; Bob Gathman and His Group Speak Easy Offer Hope to Stutterers." "Inspirations" column. *Record*, March 29, 1998.

Gold, Jeffrey. "EPA Approves 'Interim' Plan to Bury Dioxin." Associated Press. *Record*, August 6, 1998.

"High Dioxin Levels a Threat to Crabbers." *Record,* July 18, 1995.

Kelly, Mike. "A Place of Healing Hidden Scars; By Sharing Stories, Ex-POWs Cope with Lingering Trauma." "Dispatches" column. *Record,* April 13, 1998, A1.

Lifton, Robert Jay. *Home from the War, Vietnam Veterans: Neither Victims nor Executioners.* New York: Simon and Schuster, 1973.

McAleavy, Teresa. "Randy Schwartz, Fair Lawn, Photographer and Teacher." "One Life" column. *Record,* December 18, 1993.

McGrath, Mary. "On the Trail of Agent Orange; N.J. Group Tracks Birth Defects." *Record,* February 20, 1994.

Madara, Edward J. "Ideas and Considerations for Starting a Mutual Aid Self-Help Group:" *The Self-Help Sourcebook.* 4th ed. Denville, N.J.: American Self-Help Clearinghouse, 1992.

Mumma, Christopher. "Agent Orange Fight in N.J.; Vets Lobbying for State Panel." *Record,* July 29, 1993.

Rankin, Robert A., and Michael E. Ruane. "'Damage Is Already Done'; Clinton Expands Benefits for Agent Orange Victims." Knight-Ridder News Service. *Record,* May 29, 1996.

"Right All Along; Agent Orange Unmasked; New Study Links It to Three Cancers." *Record,* July 28, 1993.

"Serious Birth Defects Linked to Agent Orange." *Record,* March 15, 1996.

Shea, Kathleen. "Helping Those Who Help Themselves; Jersey Organization Serves as National Self-Help Group Clearinghouse." *Star-Ledger,* March 27, 1997, 31–32.

Smith, Jack. *Car Accident: A Practical Recovery Manual for Drivers, Passengers, and the People in Their Lives.* Cleveland, Ohio: Stress Press, 1995.

"State Disbands Agent Orange Panel." Associated Press. *Record,* July 1, 1996.

5 *Grassroots-to-Global Citizen Action*

Barry, Jan. "Activists Wage Peace . . . One Town at a Time." *Record,* August 28, 1984, A15.

———. "Enlisting City Hall in the Campaign for Peace." *Fellowship,* December 1984, 9–10.

———. "From War to Peace: Changing the Culture." *Unwinding the Vietnam War.* Seattle, Wash.: Real Comet Press, 1987.

———. *The Great Challenge: How You Can Help Prevent Nuclear War.* Montclair, N.J.: Essex County Office on Peace, 1986.

———. "'It's a Big World'; Clifton Manufacturer Reaching Out to Russia." *Record,* December 11, 1992, D1.

———. "Peace Mission to Moscow." *The Reporter* (newsletter of the Passaic County Bar Association, Paterson, N.J.), March 1987, 65, 67.

———. "US-USSR Bridges for Peace." *SANE Impact,* November–December 1986.

————, et al. *Nuclear War and Montclair: Is There a Place to Hide?*
Montclair, N.J.: Montclair Nuclear War Education Committee,
1983.
"Bridges for Peace Delegates Return." *Montclair (N.J.) Times*, Octo-
ber 9, 1986, 1.
Diaz, Willy, and Neal Allen. "A Soviet Peace Group Is Visiting in New
Jersey." *Record*, March 2, 1987, A9.
Eldridge, Douglas. "Red Carpet Out; 3 Soviet Officials Tour Town."
Montclair (N.J.) Times, July 3, 1991, A1.
Gardner, Clinton C., ed. *Building Bridges: US-USSR. A Handbook for
Citizen Diplomats*. Norwich, Vt.: Norwich Center Books, 1989.
Porter, Mark S. "Sister Cities Shine within Montclair." *Montclair (N.J.)
Times*, December 17, 1998, A3.
Pumpyansky, Alexander. Series of articles in *New Times* (Moscow),
nos. 29–32, 1987.
Stewart, Angela. "'Peace and Friendship'; Jerseyans Tell of Soviet Fear,
Puzzlement on Arms Issue." *Star-Ledger*, October 15, 1986, 16.
Terrell, Stanley E. "Montclair Man Pleasantly Surprised by Eye-open-
ing Soviet Excursion." *Star-Ledger*, November 16, 1986.

6 *Putting It All Together*

Alderson, Betty Weir. "Flunking Retirement." *Remedy*, November/
December 1998, 33.
"The Electronic Activist—Activism How-To." Institute for First
Amendment Studies (www.berkshire.net/~ifas/activist/how-to/
index.html).
Fenske, Helen. Speech at Great Swamp Watershed Annual Dinner,
November 11, 1998.
Kahn, Si. *How People Get Power*. Washington, D.C.: National Asso-
ciation of Social Workers, 1994.
————. *Organizing: A Guide for Grassroots Leaders*. Washington, D.C.:
National Association of Social Workers, 1991.
Owens, Owen D. *Living Waters: How to Save Your Local Stream*. New
Brunswick, N.J.: Rutgers University Press, 1993.

Interviews
Tittel, Jeff. Princeton, April 9, 1999.

7 *Conducting a Citizens' Campaign*

Allee, Rod. "An Environmentalist Takes Grass-Roots Fight to Higher
Level." "County Life" column. *Record*, July 12, 1998.
Barry, Jan. "Ecology Group Marks Decade on Front Lines." *Record*,
October 14, 1997, L1.
————. "'Mandate' against Sewers Will Be Heeded; Ringwood Seeking
Alternatives to Development." *Record*, November 10, 1994, C4.

———. "Ringwood Sewers Rejected." *Record*, November 9, 1994, B1.
———. "Sewerage Options in Hands of Voters; Ringwood Council OKs Referendum." *Record*, September 29, 1994, B1.
Nieves, Lisa. "CLEAN Marks 10th Anniversary Protecting the Environment." *Suburban Trends* (Butler, N.J.), October 12, 1997, A5.
Tedeschi, Bruno. "Wilderness Jewel in Peril." *Record*, February 14, 1999, A1.
Vial, Debra Lynn. "Hate Campaign Stirs Fear in Ringwood; Environmentalists Targeted." *Record*, December 10, 1993.

Interview
Tittel, Jeff. Princeton. April 9, 1999.

9 Navigating the News Media

"How to Prepare a Press Release." *The Record* and North Jersey Newspapers (Hackensack, N.J.), 1999.
Shaw, Randy. *The Activist's Handbook: A Primer for the 1990s and Beyond*. Berkeley: University of California Press, 1996.
West, Bernadette, Peter M. Sandman, and Michael R. Greenberg, eds. *The Reporter's Environmental Handbook*. New Brunswick, N.J.: Rutgers University Press, 1995.

Index

Wise Use countercampaign,
135, 136, 138
World Peacemakers, Northern
New Jersey Branch, 107
World Wide Web, 126. *See also*
Internet
writing: press releases (*see*
press releases); publicizing
goals through, 123. *See also*
publicity

Young Men's Christian
Association (YMCA), 150
Young Women's Christian
Association (YWCA), xv-
xvi, 150
and prevention of nuclear
war, 99, 100, 101

Zonenberg, Stephanie, 17, 18,
26, 27, 28–29